CW00539610

 Report

Worldviews in Religious Education

Trevor Cooling, with
Bob Bowie and Farid Panjwani

Acknowledgements

Theos would like to thank the authors for their significant time and insight in the preparation of this report, as well as Culham St Gabriel's Trust for their generous funding towards this project.

Contents

Executive Summary

Religious Education in schools is a vital means of ensuring religious literacy in any society – but in the UK, it is under threat. In a YouGov survey of the general public early in 2018, RE was in the bottom four subjects in ranking of considered importance. Only Drama, Classics, and Latin were lower.[1] In another YouGov survey later in 2018, this time of school pupils, only 12% of the 4000 surveyed pupils spread across the 6-15 age range were prepared to admit to enjoying RE a lot. In contrast, 47% enjoyed science a lot and 31% enjoyed history a lot. Only Citizenship polled lower than RE, with 6% enjoying it a lot.[2] In secondary schools there is a decline in the number of pupils entering for public examinations in Religious Studies, and an increase in the number of schools not offering the subject even though it is required by law.[3] It seems that the public think RE is an unimportant relic, pupils do not enjoy it as much as most other subjects, and secondary school students are withdrawing from taking exams in it. The stark reality is that some radical rethinking is necessary if the subject is to survive at all.

It was with this in mind that the Commission on RE (CoRE) made its landmark recommendations in 2018, in a report entitled *Religion and Worldviews: The Way Forward*. Its recommendation that the focus of the subject should now be on "worldviews" has sparked particular comment, and although the CoRE report was well received by much of the RE community itself, some groups were critical of its proposals and they have not yet been taken forward by government. This Theos report responds to these criticisms, interpreting and developing the idea of "worldview" and explores its implications for the classroom.

Chapter 1 reviews the history of RE over the last 80 years. It argues that there have been several significant shifts, or paradigm changes, in the perceived purpose of the subject in response to the changing social context in which schools exist. The shift from regarding RE as induction into the Christian heritage of the nation to seeing it as preparation for life in a religiously diverse and non-religious society has perhaps been the most significant shift so far. This chapter argues that CoRE's suggestion of a move towards "Religion and Worldviews" is another significant paradigm change in thinking about the subject, moving beyond what has become a rather arid approach to teaching world religions towards a new approach altogether.

Chapter 2 reviews three significant objections to CoRE's proposals. These are:

1. That changing the focus to worldviews introduces additional non-religious subject matter diluting the proper attention that should be given to religions.

2. That the concept of worldviews is confused and unhelpful.

3. That a focus on worldview means the true spiritual nature of the subject is lost.

In response to these objections, we argue:

1. That the worldview proposal should not be seen as a focus on the content to be taught, but as a way of framing how that content is introduced to the students.

2. That in order to understand the worldviews being taught, the focus should not be so much on the

institutional version as on the lived experience of adherents.

3. That the notion of personal worldview, with its emphasis on the heart as well as the head, needs to be central to this new approach to RE.

Chapter 3 examines the notion of understanding in RE and argues that there are two approaches to choose from. The first focuses on pupils acquiring information about worldviews whereas the second focuses on pupils learning to *interpret* the information they acquire. The latter, we argue, is the only legitimate approach if the idea of worldview is to be taken seriously. We introduce the notion of hermeneutics (the skill of interpretation), with its emphasis on understanding being about a dialogue between the pupil and the subject matter rather than simply the acquisition of information.

Chapter 4 then turns to the controversial question of how much influence those who hold to a religious worldview should have on RE. Some people argue that any religious influence is inappropriate in an educational context. We accept that such influence can be inappropriate, but this is not simply a problem for religious people. Rather it is a problem for everyone, if it is accepted that everyone has a worldview. The chapter develops the notion of responsible influence as something that people of religious faith or none should all seek to practice.

Finally, Chapter 5 concludes with three autobiographical reflections from the report's contributors. These trace how our own worldviews have developed over a lifetime and identify the religious influences and their interaction with our academic work. The chapter illustrates the powerful transformational nature of worldview in three lives and the complex interaction of factors that contribute to the development of a personal worldview. The intention is to offer a vision of the potential outcomes of an academically rigorous approach to RE that is framed by the worldview idea.

1 *www.yougov.co.uk/topics/politics/articles-reports/2018/02/15/ english-maths-science-and-computing-are-most-impor*

2 *www.yougov.co.uk/topics/education/articles-reports/2018/09/03/ which-school-subjects-do-boys-and-girls-enjoy-more*

3 For fuller details see the Commission on Religious Education (CoRE), *Religion and Worldviews: The Way Forward* (London: Religious Education Council, 2018).

Introduction

You are no doubt reading this report because you are interested in schools' Religious Education (RE). Maybe you are a teacher or someone else whose professional work involves you in RE. Or maybe you are a parent who wants to know more about the subject, possibly because you are worried what your children will be taught. Or perhaps you are involved in religious ministry in schools or serve on a Standing Advisory Council for RE (SACRE) in some capacity.[1] Or possibly you simply recognise that what we teach children about religion and belief in schools is fundamentally important to the health of society as a whole. We share your enthusiasm. RE is a really important subject.

Unfortunately, the evidence is that we enthusiasts are very much in the minority. In a YouGov survey of the general public early in 2018, RE was in the bottom four subjects in ranking of considered importance.[2] Only Drama, Classics and Latin were lower. In another YouGov survey later in 2018, this time of school pupils, only 12% of the 4000 surveyed pupils spread across the 6-15 age range were prepared to admit to enjoying RE a lot.[3] In contrast, 47% enjoyed science a lot and 31% enjoyed history a lot. Only Citizenship polled lower than RE, with 6% enjoying it a lot. In secondary schools there is a decline in the number of pupils entering for public examinations in Religious Studies, and an increase in the number of schools not offering the subject even though it is required by law.[4] It seems that the public think RE is an unimportant relic, pupils do not enjoy it as much as most other subjects and secondary school students are withdrawing from taking exams in it. The stark reality is that the subject is under threat. If it is to survive, some radical rethinking is necessary. In what follows, we will offer some developing ideas in the belief that they provide a basis for reinvigorating RE so that it becomes a subject that pupils enjoy and the general public value.

RE is unique in England and Wales, being the only subject where the syllabus is determined by a local authority. It is protected by law and should be taught in every government-funded school. However it was not included in the English Baccalaureate, the government's list of subjects that it uses to measure school performance. This omission has led to schools increasingly treating it as a less significant subject. It has also led to increased anxiety amongst RE teachers, who seek to prove its academic credibility in an attempt to persuade headteachers not to reduce the time given to it, or even to drop it altogether.

In September 2018, the RE Council of England and Wales (REC) published a significant report resulting from the deliberations of the independent Commission on RE (CoRE) that it had set up two years earlier.[5] The Commission only covered England, because the Welsh Government was conducting its own review of RE and its approach to RE is distinctively different.[6] But the Commission's report is likely to have much wider implications beyond the borders of England. A key feature of the report was its focus on "worldview" as a new idea for RE. Many of those active in RE were positive about this, but there were also some who resisted it. Here, we offer a positive interpretation and development of CoRE's advocacy of "worldview".

Chapter 1 describes the history of RE's development since the 1950s, introduces the notion of paradigm shifts in how the subject is understood and explains how CoRE's advocacy of worldview represents a new paradigm.

Chapter 2 describes and responds to various criticisms that were made of the worldview idea in the CoRE report.

Chapter 3 then offers a distinctive contribution to the debate about worldview which highlights the importance of hermeneutics (the art of interpretation) and reviews some recent resources.

Chapter 4 considers the question of whether there is a legitimate contribution to be made to RE by religious communities in the light of the new emphasis on worldview in RE.

Chapter 5 comprises three autobiographical reflections on the contribution of worldview to academic and personal development.

Note on authorship

This report is the result of co-operation between three people – Trevor Cooling, Bob Bowie and Farid Panjwani. We all work as academics and share a conviction that our personal religious faith is fundamental to our professional work as scholars of Religious Education. I, Trevor, am the main author. I have been helped greatly in my task by dialogue with Bob and Farid. They have each contributed to Chapter 5, where they, along with me, reflect on the interaction between personal worldview and academic work. In Chapter 4, Bob has also contributed a case study on his work in developing new approaches to teaching the Bible in schools. I am grateful to them for their support, but readers should be aware that only I take responsibility for the views expressed in this report, other than when Bob and Farid write in their own voices.

Some readers will know that, at the time of writing, I served as Chair of the Religious Education Council for England

and Wales (REC). I wish to stress that, in writing this report, I speak only on behalf of myself and not on behalf of the REC. At the same time, I am proud that the REC initiated, and is now promoting, the Commission on RE Report, with its particular emphasis on the new idea of worldview.

1 By law, every local authority in England and Wales is required establish a SACRE to advise it on RE. This is because, unlike any other subject, the local authority is responsible for the RE syllabus taught in its schools. Representatives of religious groups serve on SACRE by statutory requirement and, in some cases, representatives of Humanism are also appointed.

2 *www.yougov.co.uk/topics/politics/articles-reports/2018/02/15/ english-maths-science-and-computing-are-most-impor*

3 *www.yougov.co.uk/topics/education/articles-reports/2018/09/03/ which-school-subjects-do-boys-and-girls-enjoy-more*

4 For fuller details see the Commission on Religious Education (CoRE), *Religion and Worldviews: The Way Forward* (London: Religious Education Council, 2018).

5 Commission on Religious Education (CoRE), *Religion and Worldviews: The Way Forward* (London: Religious Education Council, 2018).

6 *hwb.gov.wales/curriculum-for-wales/humanities/ designing-your-curriculum/#cross-curricular-skills-and-integral-skills*

1
Paradigm changes in Religious Education

In this chapter the notion of paradigm change in RE is introduced and the changes that have taken place over the last 70 years are described. The influence of changing context on paradigm change is underlined and the link of the current context to the new emphasis on worldview is considered.

At the first meeting of the Commission, in my capacity as Chair of the REC, I challenged the commissioners to produce a "game-changer".[1] A more academic way of talking about a game-change is to refer to it as a paradigm change. This terminology became influential after Thomas Kuhn published his book *The Structure of Scientific Revolutions* in 1962.[2] In this, he challenged contemporary understanding of the nature of science by rejecting the widespread belief that it operated on the basis of continuous, objective progress. Instead, Kuhn argued that periods of normal science, where science is cumulative and progressive, are interrupted by paradigm changes, where there is a revolution in how scientists conceptualise their discipline. An example is the shift from Newtonian to Einsteinian physics.

Paradigm changes can be readily seen in the history of RE. We can start by way of an analogy by tracing the changes in school meals since the Second World War.

Paradigm changes can be readily seen in the history of RE. We can start by way of an analogy by tracing the changes in school meals since the Second World War. Older readers like me may remember the one-meal-for-all policy where everyone was expected to eat and appreciate the same food. Seared on my memory is the image of a plate with yellowing liver, lumpy mashed potato, anaemic cabbage and watery gravy, only redeemed by the jam roly-poly and custard that followed. The other image is of a fearsome dinner supervisor whose job it was to ensure we ate what was on our plate. The philosophy of school dinners was that the powers-that-be knew what was good for pupils to eat. The swill bins represented the only form of resistance.

When I started teaching in the mid-1970s, things had changed. The cafeteria system ruled. The powers-that-be had been persuaded by the swill bins. As a young, bachelor teacher I thoroughly enjoyed my daily lunch of burger, chips and beans, which I earnt by volunteering to supervise the lunch break. Most of the pupils shared my dietary preference! Pupil choice reigned. Autonomy became the hallmark of school meal philosophy.

Then Jamie Oliver came along and the third major paradigm change hit the school dinner hall. It was acknowledged that pupils did not always choose wisely or in their own best interests. Healthy eating education and "guided" choice became the hallmarks of the school canteen. What exactly that means is a work still in progress.

Within RE, it can be argued that there are similar shifts in underlying philosophy when the emphasis was on first Christian confessionalism, then on multifaith non-confessionalism and, finally, on sound personal development. As we proceed, it will quickly become obvious that things are more complex than this simple description, but this analogy works well in introducing the notion of paradigm change in RE.

First of all, in post-war Britain, RE figured significantly in the government's programme of renewal of civic spirit through education. The political consensus was that the rebuilding of a Christian nation was required. School RE syllabuses prescribed Bible knowledge to be learned as the basis of unity between the warring churches and nothing distinctive of any particular denomination was taught. The powers-that-be in our supposedly Christian nation knew what was best. This consensus was called Christian confessionalism.

However, two developments that took hold in the 1950s rocked this consensus. The first was the diversification of religion and belief communities in the country, often as a result of immigration, but also as a result of the growing civic recognition of long-existing religious minorities. Exclusively Christian RE no longer served the needs of the population. The second was an increasing recognition that RE dealt with controversial issues and there was therefore a real danger of indoctrination. In these circumstances, it was agreed that pupils should be enabled to make their own choices. The cafeteria had arrived in the RE classroom. Autonomy was the framing concept for RE. RE was now multifaith and non-confessional.

> The cafeteria had arrived in the RE classroom. Autonomy was the framing concept for RE. RE was now multifaith and non-confessional.

This was expressed through what many now call the "world religions" paradigm, which focused on ensuring that pupils had accurate information about different religious and, more recently, non-religious belief systems. At its best this introduced pupils to the reality of lived belief through carefully honing their ability to represent other people's lives in a sensitive and respectful manner, and to be aware of the dangers of stereotyping and other misrepresentation as they interpreted their beliefs. The focus was on both "learning about and learning from religion" so that pupils' personal development was promoted by what they learnt.[3] One leading academic described this as "edification".[4] Most importantly, the teacher's job was to ensure that the pupils had the information they required to make their own religious and non-religious choices in life – or, as one leading academic in RE described it, "we should seek every opportunity to strengthen young people's capacity to 'roll their own'".[5]

Then came 9/11. Even before that tragedy, it was becoming obvious that not all the religious choices that people made were good ones. The laissez-faire approach of a relativistic RE that treated all religious and non-religious beliefs as benign was not looking fit for purpose. The government launched its controversial Prevent programme against radicalisation.[6] Religious leaders wrote books such as Jonathan Sacks' *Not in God's Name*, seeking to confront the perversion of religion. RE responded in kind. The notion of helping students to make wise, educated, balanced and beneficial choices in matters of religion and belief became centre stage. However how this might be achieved was disputed. Two strands of thought gained influence.

On the one hand, in the 1990s, the notion of "experiential" RE was championed by a number of advisers and academics.[7] This focused on the inner experience of the pupil and used many techniques such as stilling and guided fantasy to engage students with their spiritual inner self.[8] On the other hand, there was a shift to the promotion of philosophy and the study of ethical issues. This was designed to promote objective, critical thinking and rational approaches to controversial and sensitive matters. Both were popular with pupils and teachers and, done well, both made important contributions. However, both approaches lost connection with the substantive content of RE – namely, religion. In the experiential approach it disappeared into a focus on pupil subjectivity and in the philosophical approach into a focus on developing thinking skills and debating issues. Religious knowledge was in danger of extinction.

Most recently, stimulated by the government's adoption of the ideas of the American educationalist ED Hirsch, attention has now shifted to academic rigour in education achieved through knowledge acquisition.[9] In particular, this has moved many in RE away from the notion of "learning from" and its accompanying emphasis on personal development to a focus on knowledge of religions and beliefs. The notion of religious literacy has become popular. This knowledge emphasis was particularly manifested in the reforms to the Religious Studies GCSE examinations that took place in 2015, in which the then Schools Minister Nick Gibb, a key advocate of Hirsch's ideas, played an active role. This was a significant intervention since it was the first time that central government had a major influence on the detail of the RE curriculum.

This brief survey indicates how the paradigm that shaped understandings of the purpose of RE in schools has changed over the last seventy years. The biggest shift was from the Christian civic religious instruction paradigm to the world religions paradigm around fifty years ago. Developments since then have mostly been variations on that world religions paradigm, which focuses on the religions as discrete, self-contained, clearly defined traditions as the main subject content. Even when Humanism is included, as it increasingly is, the approach taken to it mirrors the world religions paradigm. Approaches which have departed from this model, such as the shift to experience or to philosophy described earlier, have rather lost touch with religion. In what follows, I will argue that the CoRE report encapsulates another fundamental paradigm shift, where the idea of worldview is central but a clear focus on religion is maintained.

The current context

The paradigm changes in RE that I have described were responses to changing social contexts. What then of our current context? The British Social Attitudes Survey published in September 2018 spelled out the issue in two stark sentences: "70% of those aged 18-24 say they have no religion. This is an increase from 56% in 2002".[10] This 70% are the so-called "nones". Other research indicates the demographic landscape in which RE sits is changing dramatically with a marked decline in the influence of institutional Christianity, a rise in new and varied spiritualities, and resurgence amongst a few in more radical forms of religious commitment.[11] This means that the context that RE teachers work in is now quite different from fifty years ago when the world religions paradigm emerged. First, the potential content to include in the curriculum is vast and complex if it is to include all the major traditions now represented in Britain. That makes content selection potentially unmanageable. Second, it is likely that the pupil clientele teachers work with has diminishing interest in the traditional world religions paradigm because of its sole focus on institutional religions.

The situation is worrying. RE has become disconnected from

The attempt to make the subject spiritual led it away from knowledge of religion. The attempt to make it more academic ended up making it mainly about philosophy. The attempt to study all religions led it into rather superficial caricatures and generalisations and overloaded the curriculum.

the pupils and the "real religious landscape".[12] The attempt to make the subject spiritual led it away from knowledge of religion. The attempt to make it more academic ended up making it mainly about philosophy. The attempt to study all religions led it into rather superficial caricatures and generalisations and overloaded the curriculum.

A new paradigm is needed. I will argue that the notion of worldview offers exciting new possibilities; an approach that is both academically rigorous and meaningful for all pupils, be they religious or nones.

The Commission on RE: introducing worldview

There is no comparable organisation to the REC anywhere else in the world.[13] I vividly recall once explaining it to the Archbishop of Sydney whilst enjoying the growing look of astonishment on his face.

The REC is the umbrella organisation that brings together all the associations, bodies and societies that have an interest in supporting RE in schools. These include both faith and belief communities, from Anglicans to Zoroastrians, and professional organisations from advisers to teachers. It boasts the most extraordinarily diverse membership that reflects the changing landscape of religion and belief in Britain. In 2016, in response to the increasingly perilous state of RE as a subject in schools, the REC established the independent Commission on Religious Education (CoRE). Fourteen commissioners were appointed and their final report was launched at the House of Commons in September 2018.[14]

At the heart of the CoRE report is concern about the inequality experienced by pupils in England given the very different provision for RE that exists across the country.[15]

There are of course some excellent examples of very good provision and teaching. However, the overall picture is patchy and deteriorating. Furthermore, the commissioners took very seriously the need to respond to the changing belief demographic of young people and the changing status of religion in society. They accepted the judgment that:

> *It is really important to grasp these changes because there is a real religion and belief landscape, and there is one imagined by the policy-makers, and there is a growing gap between them.*[16]

The commissioners wanted to ensure that all pupils in England experienced high quality RE taught by well-qualified teachers, which they found personally inspiring irrespective of their own personal commitment. Their solution was to call for a legislated National Entitlement in Religion and Worldviews applicable to all schools, embodying the aspiration that all pupils develop a good understanding of the role that worldviews, be they religious or non-religious, play in human life. The focus on worldview was intended to make RE more inclusive and relevant and the accompanying National Entitlement, a set of statements explaining what all pupils are entitled to experience in RE, was designed to redress the inequalities in pupils' experience of RE.

So what did the commissioners mean by *worldview*? A straightforward way of thinking about it is to describe it as constituting both the conscious and the hidden assumptions that people and communities hold. In

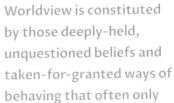

Worldview is constituted by those deeply-held, unquestioned beliefs and taken-for-granted ways of behaving that often only come to the forefront of our attention when they are challenged in some way.

other words, worldview is constituted by those deeply-held, unquestioned beliefs and taken-for-granted ways of behaving that often only come to the forefront of our attention when they are challenged in some way. My favourite expression to describe them is offered by the Australian educator, Professor Brian Hill. He calls them RIBs (reasonable initial bets).[17] The commissioners' attempt at defining worldview was:

> [A] person's way of understanding, experiencing and responding to the world. It can be described as a philosophy of life or an approach to life. This includes how a person understands the nature of reality and their own place in the world. A person's worldview is likely to influence and be influenced by their beliefs, values, behaviours, experiences, identities and commitments...[18]

This new approach does not entail, as some suppose, just a study of ideas because "learning about a worldview without reference to the lived experience of adherents... is insufficient for effective learning". Furthermore, given the changing demography of the country, the commissioners recommend that both religious and non-religious worldviews should be studied. For some, this extension of the subject beyond religion is a controversial proposal.[19] In contrast, the commissioners see the classroom as a safe environment in which the challenging reality of diversity of belief and practice in society can be explored by pupils.

The CoRE report distinguishes between what it calls institutional or organised worldviews, like Christianity, Sikhism and Humanism, which not everyone identifies with, and personal or individual worldviews, which everyone has (or perhaps it is better to say *inhabits*). It asserts that "everyone has a worldview", because we all seek to make sense of life even though we may not be able to articulate our worldview in a coherent way or even be conscious of its impact in our lives. The aspiration is that this new approach to RE is relevant to everyone, including the increasing number of pupils who do not themselves identify with a particular faith or belief community, because they too have a worldview – even if not an institutionally endorsed one. CoRE did not pursue the pedagogical implications of the distinction between these two understandings of worldview. However, it was clear in its aspiration that the purpose of studying institutional worldviews is both "to enable each pupil to understand, reflect on and develop their own personal worldview" and to "understand the worldviews of others".

The CoRE Report is a huge achievement; it marks the beginning of a paradigm change in RE, but it is not the finished product.[20] It has suggested a possible adjustment to the tiller that sets the subject in a new direction, but what this might mean in practice is not yet clear. We will pick up these matters in later chapters.

1   Amira Tharani, 'The Commission on Religious Education' in Mark Chater (ed),
    Reforming RE: Power and Knowledge in a Worldviews Curriculum (Woodbridge: John
    Catt, 2020), p. 39.

2   Thomas Kuhn, *The Structure of Scientific Revolutions* (Chicago: University of
    Chicago Press, 1962).

3   The phrase "learning about and learning from religion" was coined by
    Michael Grimmitt and became influential through his book *Religious Education
    and Human Development* (Great Wakering: McCrimmons, 1987). It was used
    extensively by teachers to describe the purpose of RE until quite recently.

4   Robert Jackson, Religious Education: an interpretive approach (London:
    Hodder & Stoughton, 1997) p. 130-134.

5   Michael Grimmitt, *Religious Education and Human Development* (Great Wakering:
    McCrimmons, 1987) p. 208.

6   Jonathan Sacks, *Not in God's Name: Confronting Religious Violence* (London,
    Hodder & Stoughton, 2015). For the Prevent programme see *www.gov.uk/
    government/publications/prevent-duty-guidance*

7   John Hammond et al., *New Methods in Religious Education Teaching: An Experiential
    Approach* (London: Oliver & Boyd, 1990).

8   These are exercises where the teacher creates activities that enable pupils to
    develop their spirituality. Today, these would probably be seen as mindfulness
    techniques.

9   Nick Gibb, 'How E. D. Hirsch Came to Shape UK Government Policy' in
    Jonathan Simons and Natasha Porter (eds.), *Knowledge and the Curriculum*
    (London: Policy Exchange, 2015).

10 *natcen.ac.uk/news-media/press-releases/2018/september/
    church-of-england-numbers-at-record-low/*

11 Linda Woodhead and Rebecca Catto, *Religion and Change in Modern Britain*
    (Abingdon: Routledge, 2012).

12 Adam Dinham and Martha Shaw, *RE for REal*, (London: Goldsmiths, University
    of London, 2015).

13 *www.religiouseducationcouncil.org.uk/*

14 CoRE, *Religion and Worldviews: the Way Forward*, (London, REC, 2018).

15 National Association of Teachers of Religious Education (NATRE), *The State of
    the Nation: A report on the provision of Religious Education within secondary schools in
    England* (Birmingham: NATRE, 2018).

16 Adam Dinham and Martha Shaw, 'Landscapes, Real and Imagined: RE for Real'
    in Mark Chater, *Reforming...* p. 53.

17 Brian Hill, *Exploring Religion in School: A National Priority* (Adelaide: Openbook Publishers, 2004).

18 CoRE, *Religion and...* p. 4.

19 See for example L. Philip Barnes, *Crisis, Controversy and the Future of Religious Education* (Abingdon: Routledge, 2019).

20 The Religious Education Council is undertaking follow up projects to develop the implications for the classroom.

2
Criticisms and defence of the "worldview" approach

This chapter examines and responds to three criticisms that were made of CoRE's use of worldview and then offers three refinements of the idea in an attempt to take the conversation forward.

Concerns about the worldview approach

Whilst the CoRE Report was welcomed by many people, there were a number of critical responses to the recommendation that there should be a worldview focus to RE. Three are of significance for our discussion: what we shall call the "subject content" objection, the "conceptual" objection, and the "human" objection.

a) The subject content objection

This objection was basically that the proposed change introduces *additional* subject matter into RE, namely worldviews, where worldviews are taken to be a distinct category of extra non-religious content over and above the many religions already being studied. This interpretation was fuelled by the support given to the CoRE Report by Humanists UK, which has argued over many years for the systematic study of Humanism alongside the religions. Their website welcomes the Report because it "proposes to rename the subject 'religion and worldviews' in order to make explicit that humanism must be taught on an equal footing to religions".[1]

CoRE's proposed worldview paradigm seeks to replace the current world religions paradigm by reframing the way that content should be taught.

The critics regard this perceived attempt to add non-religious content as an inappropriate dilution of the proper focus of RE on religion. The objection was that worldviews like Humanism, the main contender for inclusion, can be studied elsewhere in the curriculum, but that RE should be reserved for the study of religions. Furthermore, as we have already indicated, the diversity of religious and non-religious communities in England is such that it was feared that this addition of yet more content in the cause of fairly representing all these communities would make the subject content unmanageable and create impossible expectations. No doubt, many RE teachers and syllabus writers would share this concern, given the small amount of curriculum time generally allocated to RE.

This objection assumes, therefore, that the word "worldviews" refers solely to the addition of non-religious belief positions to the content to be studied. Not surprisingly, it came largely from faith communities.[2] Both the faith community objectors and Humanist supporters regard this as a victory for Humanism in the battle for space on the RE curriculum.

However, this is a misreading of the CoRE Report, which is not primarily concerned with adding non-religious content (which it takes for granted as already part of a good RE programme). Rather, CoRE proposes a significant *reframing* of RE in terms of understanding worldview as a shared human phenomenon, of which there are religious and non-religious manifestations.[3] Both parties in this debate are reading the CoRE Report through the lens of the world religions paradigm. That is a fundamental error. The new worldview paradigm offers a wholly new perspective, not simply yet more subject content. The crucial difference is that the world religions paradigm assumes that RE is solely about knowledge of religions and Humanism with the focus on the study of the (unfortunately too often stereotypically represented) lives of believers. In contrast, the proposed worldview paradigm assumes that RE is about knowledge of how worldview is important in human life with the focus on the study of the lives of all human beings, including the worldview influences on the pupils, but with a particular focus on religion and its alternatives.

b) The conceptual objection

The conceptual objection focuses on the definition of the word "worldview". One version is exemplified in the writings of Michael Hand, a professor at the University of Birmingham who challenged CoRE's assertion that everyone has a worldview.[4] His argument was that worldview is a concept that only applies to people who identify with institutionalised religions. In responding specifically to CoRE, Hand asserted that the switch to worldviews "is a deeply unhelpful suggestion" and further argued that the notion of worldview is mistakenly applied in the examples of the non-religious worldviews given in the CoRE report. He argues that: "A worldview is, roughly, a theory of the meaning of life, an account of the significance, origin, and purpose of human existence", which applies to religions, but to say that everyone has a worldview "looks very much like the imposition on non-believers of a category developed with believers in mind". Andrew Copson of Humanists UK advanced a similar argument in his response to CoRE, arguing:

> The identification of atheism, agnosticism, and secularism as non-religious worldviews is a disappointing conceptual confusion that we would have hoped the Commission would avoid. All three should of course be studied in the subject in detail, but they are not worldviews. Atheism and agnosticism are simple positions on the existence or otherwise of gods, and they are no more non-religious worldviews than theism is a religion. Secularism is

*(depending on the academic field) either a political philosophy
that can be held by religious and non-religious alike or a
sociological description of a certain social approach associated
with modernity. Either way, it is not a non-religious worldview in
that way that humanism or nihilism are.*[5]

Both Copson and Hand appear to want worldview to be
a tightly defined concept that captures what CoRE calls an
institutional worldview. Their motivation is different; Hand is
critical of the CoRE Report and Copson welcomes it, but their
call for conceptual clarity is intended, in both cases, to limit the
field of study. This goes against the clearly stated intentions
of CoRE, which advocated a fluid and open understanding of
worldview in its full diversity. There are viable alternatives to
this tight definition approach that embrace all people and are
more credible. We will explore such later in this chapter.

Another version of the conceptual objection is raised
by Todd Weir in a TED talk.[6] He expresses concerns about
the associations provoked by the term and argues that the
worldview concept encourages a tribal mentality that thinks
in "them and us terms" and does not encourage the open and
cooperative approach that is essential for education in healthy
democracies. Instead, it evokes notions of conflicting and
oppositional, closed and systematised tribal ideologies that are
resistant to change and can easily become totalitarian. "I am
this and always will be; you are that and always will be; we are,
therefore, in conflict".[7]

This is clearly a legitimate concern. The last thing CoRE
was proposing was an approach to RE that encourages students
to decide which tribe they want to belong to and then teaches
them to defend that to the end. But worldviews do not have to
be held in this way and are certainly described in very different

terms in the CoRE Report. For me, this realisation came when I read George Marsden's history of Fuller Theological Seminary in the USA, founded by an influential American radio evangelist. In it, Marsden demonstrates how what initially was an institution seeking to defend a tribal, fundamentalist worldview can reform from within to be more open and dialogical.[8] This possibility needs to be pursued in the way RE is taught.

Hand is correct to point out that CoRE did not articulate its understanding of the term clearly enough. Weir too is correct in pointing out the danger of "totality thinking", where, to quote another author, "worldview becomes the fence that keeps you penned in and inhibits creativity" and justifies the marginalisation of others in "ideological power grabs".[9] However, the question is whether the term *has* to be understood in these negative ways; this report argues that it can, and should, be given new understandings and a fresh lease of life.

c) The human objection

The third objection derives from a major worry about the picture of what it means to be a human being that is promulgated by CoRE's focus on worldview. Thus Patricia Hannam and Gert Biesta argue that CoRE's fundamental error is to emphasise *understanding* of worldviews, thereby reducing the teacher to the level of a technician whose job is to find the right way to deliver the specified knowledge content to be understood, namely the beliefs and practices of the worldviews being studied. This means that "the child or young person is mainly positioned as an 'understander' or interpreter of things others put before them". This, they argue, is educationally inadequate because it does not promote children gaining a perspective on their own worldview and making important judgements as to whether or not it will help them to flourish in life. Faith and spirituality, they argue, have disappeared from the subject.[10] This charge, that CoRE's adoption of the language of worldview reveals an *exclusive* concern with the transmission of the content to be taught at the expense of the pupils' spiritual development, seems unfair in light of its identifying the importance of personal worldview. What is true is that CoRE did not elaborate on this notion enough. We will return to that task in due course.

Although not in direct response to CoRE, the influential Canadian-American Christian philosopher James K.A. Smith raises similar concerns about the enthusiasm for promoting a Christian worldview and of the aspiration that students develop a Christian mind that he finds in his own Christian Reformed tradition. He argues that such a focus makes an *anthropological* mistake because it treats the human person as "fundamentally a thinking thing – a cognitive machine" or, more evocatively, as "brains on sticks". This, Smith despairs, leads to an educational approach which relies on "a steady diet of ideas fed somewhat intravenously into the mind through lines of propositions and information".[11] In his view a proper worldview education should develop the students' desires and imagination, not just their cognition.

The problem, I suggest, that these critics have correctly identified is the *apparently unexamined* assumption that to teach worldview as CoRE suggests is to engage students in a spectator sport, which entails them learning stuff about a range of institutional worldviews, but nothing about themselves as spiritual beings inhabiting a worldview. This is the mistake that Hand and Copson also make in thinking that CoRE is purely focused on study of self-contained worldviews like Humanism and Christianity. It ignores the emphasis that CoRE gives to education in personal worldview.

In the rest of this chapter, I will offer a very different interpretation of CoRE's vision that will reject the content objection, correct the conceptual objection and embrace the human objection. In the course of this, I will offer a new understanding of worldview which I hope will refine CoRE's proposals.

Embracing a worldview approach

The question is then, given that there still seems to be significant debate around the term worldview, what exactly might a worldview approach to RE look like? Here CoRE provides three important insights that we can build on in order to explore further what this proposed paradigm change means in practice.

a) Worldview: more framing than content

CoRE's proposed worldview paradigm seeks to replace the current world religions paradigm (with its emphasis on learning increasing numbers of different world religions and, sometimes, Humanism) that is currently dominant in England. However, CoRE does not do this by expanding the content, but by reframing the way that content should be taught through setting out a statement of National Entitlement.[12] This includes nine statements on the learning that all pupils are entitled to experience (plus one to do with the quality of teachers they meet in RE). For example:

> Pupils must be taught the ways in which worldviews develop in interaction with each other, have some shared beliefs and practices as well as differences and that people may draw upon more than one tradition.

This illustrates that the National Entitlement is not about adding content; it does not conform to the world religions paradigm. Rather it seeks to frame the teaching of that content in such a way that pupils come to understand how worldview works in human life. In the case of this particular statement, the focus is on helping pupils understand that both institutional and personal worldviews develop through complex interactions with many influences. Successful teaching of this statement can be achieved through a systematic study of one religion or through a thematic study of many religions. Or indeed it can also be achieved through a study of ethical and philosophical issues. Adopting the National Entitlement does not therefore mean binning one's curriculum and knowledge organisers (although these documents should change in any review as teachers themselves develop in their understanding). Rather it means a new way of framing the implementation of those documents in the classroom – and this should particularly lead to changes in the learning and assessment tasks that pupils undertake and the focal questions that they engage with.

One recent and significant development that resonates with this approach is a renewed focus on the importance of disciplinary knowledge, which is distinguished from the information (the technical term is substantive content) about the worldviews taught in class.[13] By disciplinary knowledge is meant the approach that is used to study that information, which entails asking particular types of question and using a particular methodology to do that. We might call it a particular way of knowing. For example, science is a discipline because it uses controlled experiments to explore questions of cause and effect. That discipline can be used to study different types of information (biology, physics, chemistry etc.), but to learn science is to learn how to work within that discipline and not solely to absorb scientific information.

In the case of RE, teachers are beginning to explore what this means in practice. One version of this approach has suggested that there are three main disciplines relevant to RE – namely theology, philosophy and human/social sciences.[14] Another project deriving from Exeter University has pioneered resources based around cartoon characters such as "Debate-it-all Derek", "Have-a-go-Hugo" and "Ask-it-all-Ava" that enable pupils to experience some of the different disciplinary approaches that can be used in studying worldviews by identifying with the characters.[15] However it is early days as academics and teachers explore exactly which disciplines are best used in RE, and how. CoRE, however, is clear that the worldview approach will require engagement with a wide range of academic disciplines. Its contribution to this debate is the Statement of National Entitlement. It aims to shift teachers' focus of attention from the mass of information that they could potentially teach about religious and non-religious worldviews to a set of key foci to explore regarding how worldview works in human life. The important point is that the disciplines are used to plan pupils' learning about the nine elements of the National Entitlement statement. The attention should not just be on the information to learn about particular worldviews, but on learning how to investigate the way worldviews work in human life whilst studying that information.[16] A worldview approach does not simply provide new content, but rather offers a new disciplinary framing for how that content is studied through the Statement of National Entitlement.

b) Worldview: more organised than institutional

One of the consequences of the government's emphasis on knowledge (by which is usually meant information) is that the currently dominant world religions paradigm has often been reduced to the study of "organised worldviews shared amongst particular groups and sometimes embedded in institutions". The danger is that this presents the worldviews studied as discrete, sealed-box systems and implies an essentialised picture of the worldview in question meaning that pupils don't realise that there can be significant variation within that worldview. For me this point was brought home vividly during a research focus group with year 7 students at a Catholic secondary school that went like this:

> Researcher: Are you all Catholics here?
> Pupil: Oh yes, of course.
> Researcher: Do you all believe in God?
> Pupils: No (with an implied "why would we?").

As Freathy and John show in their significant article on the Report, CoRE clearly rejects this sealed-box conception of worldviews.[17] It argues that institutional worldviews are "complex, diverse and plural", "that they have changed over time" and that there are "interactions and blurred boundaries" between them. CoRE rejects the notion that worldviews are exclusively propositional in nature, instead claiming that they have "emotional, affiliative (belonging) and behavioural dimensions" and should not be reduced simply to "belief and practice". The problem with earlier approaches to RE, CoRE says, is that this reality has been largely ignored, which has "inadvertently reinforced stereotypes about religions, rather than challenging them". In contrast, CoRE urges giving attention to the varied, lived experience of people that identify with a particular institutionalised worldview and not just to an essentialised, officially sanctioned version. One thing that is absolutely clear is that CoRE rejects the pillarised[18] understanding of worldviews that some seem to assume it advocates, and embraces a much more fluid and developmental understanding of their nature. The experience of many believers can often be very different from the stereotypical presentations in textbooks and the diversity exemplified by adherents can often be at odds with the institutional presentation.[19]

This is not meant to imply that it is not possible to give an accurate overview of a particular institutional understanding of a tradition, but it does underline the danger of presenting pupils with what sounds like an authoritative description when it may only reflect one particular strand or even be a stereotype. Some therefore find that the idea of *family resemblance* is a helpful way of thinking about the relationship between the essentials of a tradition and the varied ways that these are experienced by believers. People know that they belong to their family, but their experience of belonging may be very different from, say, their other siblings. Good RE captures that sense that there are identifiable worldviews but that personal experience of being part of them may be very diverse.

Given CoRE's emphasis on the importance of studying the lived experiences of adherents rather than pre-packaged distillations provided by institutions, it seems more appropriate to describe this dimension of the content of RE as the study of organised worldviews where people have a strong identification with certain group expressions of worldviews, and to drop the language of *institutional* worldviews, with its possible implication of one monolithic expression determined by centralised authorities.

A significant contributor to current RE is Robert Jackson.[20] His work was shaped by the discipline of ethnography, which emphasised careful attention being given to the representation of adherents' experiences and perspectives. Jackson's suggestion was that an organised worldview should not be represented as homogenous, but that the lived experience of adherents should be investigated by exploring the relationships within their community, the membership groups that they identify with, and their interactions with the wider organised tradition. This reflects CoRE's concern that pupils engage with the complexity of organised worldviews rather than essentialised and often stereotypical portrayals of monolithic traditions.

c)   Worldview: more personal than individual

As we have seen, CoRE is not just concerned with organised worldviews, but also with personal or individual worldviews. A personal worldview is defined as "an individual's own way of understanding and living in the world, which may or may not draw from one, or many, institutional worldviews". When explaining this notion, CoRE focuses on the process of "making sense of life and meaning of experience". This, it is claimed, may happen at a more or less conscious level, but a core task of education is "to enable each pupil to understand, reflect on and develop their own personal worldview". Frustratingly, little more is said about personal worldview.[21]

An important question about personal worldview formation is how much happens at the conscious level and how much is unconscious response to peer, media and other pressures that are inherent in the experience of growing up. An interesting example is the influence of various intellectual movements like instrumentalism, consumerism, post-modernism and scientism. Sometimes authors speak of these as worldviews in their own right, but this is probably unhelpful in the RE classroom as they are clearly not the same as either organised or personal worldviews.[22] It seems to me that they are therefore unlikely to appear on the curriculum as explicit subjects for study in their own right in the way that Judaism or Sikhism might. But they are important *influences* on how both personal and organised worldviews develop and pupils' attention should be drawn to their role in worldview formation. For example, phenomena like prosperity theology and the vast wealth accumulated by some religious leaders are good examples of how an attachment to consumerism can be absorbed into a worldview.

To take another example, a colleague of mine, Berry Billingsley, has demonstrated the widespread influence amongst young people of the apparently unquestioned epistemic belief that science and religion inevitably clash with each other.[23] It appears that this epistemological mindset is significant in the development of young people's personal worldviews, leading to tacit difficulties with taking the study of religion seriously. This intellectual mindset will also need to be part of the rigorous academic study of organised worldviews in the classroom, because they are also influenced by it.[24]

Another of my colleagues, Ann Casson, studied pupils in Catholic schools as part of her doctoral research, to try and understand the relationship between pupils' personal worldviews and the organised worldview of the school. She found that, in this strongly institutional religious context, pupils behave as what she termed "bricoleurs" – those who construct bricolage, that is art created from a mix of different types of media and objects – constructing their own personal understandings of what it means to be Catholic in response to the nurturing attempts of the educational hierarchy of Catholicism.[25] It appears that pupils learn to become skilled cultural navigators as they bring together the varied conscious and unconscious influences on them from home, peer group, school and Church in the formation of their own personal worldviews. As I shared in my own example of conversation with Catholic pupils, my assumption that they all believed in God was mistaken. From *their* perspective, good Catholic pupils could be atheists. Being Catholic was about belonging to a cultural group, and not so much about believing religious doctrines, and that cultural group included friends who were atheists. This suggests that our personal worldview reflects the communities that have shaped us as well as the choices we make about what to believe. In the light of this insight, I suggest the term personal worldview is preferable to individual worldview, since it captures better the impact of the relational impact of living in community on worldview formation.

What is important for now when talking about personal worldviews is to shift the focus on the head that has so often dominated the discussion to embrace the heart and, particularly, to capture the importance of community in the development of a personal worldview.[26] In this respect I suggest that phrases such as "everyone has a world view", implying it is like a set of keys that we carry in our pockets, should be replaced by something like "everyone *inhabits* a worldview", which captures the tacit influence that is associated with personal worldviews.

Hopefully, Religious Education helps pupils to become self-aware and reflexive interpreters of the knowledge they gain in their classrooms.

Hopefully, Religious Education helps pupils to become self-aware and reflexive interpreters of the knowledge they gain in their classrooms. Through gaining knowledge of organised worldviews, maybe they can take more responsibility for the personal worldview that they inhabit. That is why the promotion of critical thinking is so important. Perhaps the job of RE is to support students in becoming educated bricoleurs in the development of their own personal worldview rather than the impulsive bricoleurs that it is so easy to be?

Conclusion

"Worldview" has proved to be a controversial term. It is understood differently by different people. In some significant ways it conjures up unhelpful associations, of which three are reviewed in this chapter. I have, in response, outlined three clarifications of the CoRE proposals that I trust take forward understanding of this idea. The problem is that there is not an immediately obvious alternative word to worldview that would gain traction in schools and overcome the anxieties of the critics. Instead then, my strategy in this chapter has been to redeem the term by seeking to clarify and transform what is understood by using worldview in RE.

1 *humanism.org.uk/campaigns/schools-and-education/school-curriculum/religious-education/* See also Luke Donnellan, 'What do we mean by worldview?' in Mark Chater, *Reforming...* pp. 126-130.

2 See Rob Freathy and Helen John, 'Worldviews and Big Ideas: A Way Forward for Religious Education?', Nordidactia 4 (2019). who discuss this objection from the Catholic Education Service and the Board of Deputies of British Jews. It should be noted however that the Church of England supported the CoRE Report.

3 See Religious Studies Project, RE Commission Report: A Way Forward? 2018. *www.religiousstudiesproject.com/podcast/re-commission-report-a-way-forward/*

4 Michael Hand, 'What's in a worldview? On Trevor Cooling's "Doing God in education"' *Oxford Review of Education* 38:5 (2012) pp. 527-538 and 'Why "Religion and Worldviews" is a non-starter.' *blog.bham.ac.uk/socialsciencesbirmingham/2018/10/10/religion-and-world-views/*

5 *humanism.org.uk/2018/09/09/humanists-uk-welcomes-landmark-commission-on-re-recommending-new-subject-religion-and-worldviews/*

6 See Todd Weir 'What's In A Worldview?' *www.youtube.com/watch?v=0I6LAYwN3Jk*

7 Alan Thomson, 'Worldview: Some Unanswered Questions', *Journal of Education and Christian Belief* 16:2 (2012), pp. 179-194.

8 George Marsden, *Reforming Fundamentalism: Fuller Seminary and the New Evangelicalism* (Grand Rapids, MI: Wm.B. Eerdmans Publishing Company, 1987).

9 Brian Walsh, "'Transformation: Dynamic Worldview or Repressive Ideology?' *Journal of Education and Christian* Belief 4:2 (2000), pp. 101-114.

10 Patricia Hannam and Gert Biesta, 'Religious education, a matter of understanding? Reflections on the final report of the Commission on Religious Education' *Journal of Beliefs and Values* 40:1 (2019), p. 59.

11 James K.A. Smith, *Desiring the Kingdom (Cultural Liturgies): Worship, Worldview and Cultural Formation* (Grand Rapids, MI: Baker Academics, 2009), p. 42.

12 CoRE, *Religion and...* pp. 12-13. The National Entitlement appears to have been inspired by the *Big Ideas Project. See Barbara Wintersgill* (ed), *Big Ideas for Religious Education* (Exeter: University of Exeter, 2017).

13 See Richard Kueh, 'Religious Education and the 'Knowledge Problem' in Mike Castelli and Mark Chater (eds), *We Need to Talk about Religious Education* (London: Jessica Kingsley, 2017), pp. 53-70 and 'Disciplinary hearing: Making the case for the disciplinary in Religion and Worldviews' in Mark Chater (ed), *Reforming...*, pp.131-148.

14 Gillian Georgios and Kathryn Wright 'Disciplinarity, religion and worldviews: Making the case for theology, philosophy and human/social sciences' in Mark Chater (ed), *Reforming...*, pp.149-164.

15 *www.reonline.org.uk/re-searchers-approach/*

16 This is called the development of metacognition. See Shirley Larkin, Rob Freathy, Jonathan Doney and Giles Freathy, *Metacognition, Worldviews and Religious Education: A Practical Guide for Teachers*, (Abingdon: Routledge, 2019).

17 See Rob Freathy & Helen C. John, 'Worldview and Big Ideas...'

18 This is a Dutch term describing a social system where people learn in an institution that reflects their own worldview. It is inspired by the thinking of Abraham Kuyper, a former Dutch prime minister and acclaimed social reformer in the Reformed Christian movement.

19 Robert Jackson, Julia Ipgrave, Mary Hayward, Paul Hopkins, Nigel Fancourt, Mandy Robbins, Leslie Francis and Ursula McKenna, *Materials used to Teach About World Religions in Schools in England* (Warwick: University of Warwick, 2010).

20 Robert Jackson, *Religious Education: an interpretive approach* (London: Hodder Education, 1997).

21 CoRE, *Religion and Worldviews*, p.4-7.

22 Simon Smart, *A Spectator's Guide to Worldviews: Ten Ways of Understanding Life* (Sydney: Blue Bottle Books, 2007).

23 Berry Billingsley, 'Teaching and Learning about Epistemic Insight' *School Science Review*, 365 (2017), pp. 59-64.

24 For example, this is presented as a fundamental tenet of Humanism. See *www.youtube.com/watch?v=Yk5IWzTfWeM*

25 A bricoleur is someone who constructs their own personal understanding rather than following a party line. See Ann Casson, *Fragmented Catholicity and Social Cohesion: Faith Schools in a Plural Society* (Oxford: Peter Lang, 2012).

26 See James K.A. Smith, *Desiring the Kingdom (Cultural Liturgies): Worship, Worldview and Cultural Formation* (Grand Rapids, MI: Baker Academics, 2009) pp. 65-70 and Imagining the Kingdom: How Worship Works (Grand Rapids, MI: Baker Academic, 2013) for extensive discussion of this point.

3
A distinctive contribution to the debate about worldview

In this chapter we examine two conceptions of what might be meant by developing understanding in RE. It is argued that only one of these, which highlights the role of interpretation in learning, is fit for purpose in an approach focused on worldview. Its characteristics are then explored. Finally four recently published resources are reviewed, both to illustrate this approach and to evaluate how far they succeed in achieving it.

There is one thing that is widely agreed about RE in schools – namely, that there is much disagreement. In particular there is a vigorous debate over its purpose. When teachers talk about this you will hear them mentioning, among others: the promotion of tolerance and community cohesion; the development of theological, religious or worldview literacy; the gaining of essential cultural knowledge; and the formation of character dispositions. Do teachers just take their pick?

In recent years, the influence of MP and Schools Minister Nick Gibb (see page 24) has promoted increased conversation around the importance of promoting academic rigour, which is usually interpreted as knowledge acquisition. In this relatively new climate, to seek to promote the spiritual, moral, social and cultural development of pupils is increasingly seen as the soft end of education and not part of an academic approach to RE. This is despite the fact that such promotion is a legal obligation for schools. In RE today, it seems that academic knowledge is increasingly the name of the game, particularly for secondary school teachers.

The question is, however, what do we mean by academic knowledge? I will now argue that there is a fundamentally important but largely unrecognised conflict between two basic views of what knowledge, rationality and understanding

> There is a fundamentally important but largely unrecognised conflict between two basic views of what knowledge, rationality and understanding mean in RE; is it primarily about rational objectivity or primarily about wise interpretation?

mean in RE; is it primarily about rational objectivity or primarily about wise interpretation?[1] To put it bluntly, RE teachers have to choose between these two views – and, if the worldview notion is to be at the heart of RE, I suggest only one choice is appropriate.[2] Central to my argument will be the proposal that Religion and Worldviews teaching will need to adopt a hermeneutical approach if it is to do justice to CoRE's aspired shift to the worldview paradigm.

Understanding as the aim of RE

Seeking to offer clarity, RE Adviser Kate Christopher has recently suggested that there is one single and straightforward aim in teaching Religion and Worldviews that should have sovereignty: namely, understanding.[3] This sounds an attractive and straightforward proposition that every teacher will comprehend. Unfortunately, it masks a significant dispute about what exactly we mean by "understanding" and its relationship to knowledge. A shared language which masks a significant difference of opinion is a problem waiting in the wings.

View 1: knowledge and understanding as rational objectivity

The elevation of knowledge acquisition as the goal of education reflects one end of the spectrum in this debate. In this view, understanding amounts to *mastery* of the corpus of knowledge that makes up the academic subject being studied. That knowledge is treated as largely uncontroversial; achieving academic rigour in teaching focuses on raising the demand level of the knowledge being learnt. This is what happened in the reform of GCSE Religious Studies in 2015. Effective transmission of that knowledge becomes the key pedagogical concern and increasingly teachers turn to neuroscience for insights into how to improve knowledge retention and recall by their pupils' brains.

Furthermore, knowledge acquisition is largely valued for utilitarian reasons by schools and parents because it raises test and exam performance, thereby enhancing the school's reputation and improving pupils' career prospects. In the longer term, it is valued because it is assumed to contribute to economic and scientific progress or because it enables pupils to function well as citizens. This is particularly important in politicians' eyes. Skills may also be considered important, particularly knowing how to apply the knowledge that has been mastered, but personal development is not considered to be a priority, only a welcome by-product.

Some readers of the previous paragraph will argue this is a parody, an Aunt Sally construed to prove a contrary point. I agree; guilty as charged. This is a simplification of a complex position. However, it is a fair representation of the education philosophy promulgated by influential people. It currently has a significant influence on teachers' thinking. Its particular importance is that it excludes the personal from ideas of knowledge or understanding. Applied to the teaching of Religion and Worldviews, this mindset treats understanding as straightforward, namely mastery of a knowledge base about different religious and non-religious worldviews. This reflects where the world religions paradigm has gone wrong.

We have already seen that Nick Gibb credits the work of American educationalist ED Hirsch as being the main influence on him (see page 24). Hirsch's views reflect those of Paul Hirst, a philosopher of education who was active in the 1960s and 1970s and whose ideas are still influential today.[4] Both these educationalists share the view that knowledge is publicly specifiable and objective. Sophisticated education, as Hirst calls it, inducts pupils into this objective approach to understanding. The notion of personal knowledge or worldview would be anathema for Hirst. To induct pupils into a worldview would, Hirst argues, constitute a primitive approach to education. Although most teachers would never have heard of Hirst, many are unconsciously absorbing his ideas under the influence of the world religions knowledge paradigm. In this, understanding in RE focuses on objective learning of information about the beliefs and practices of a range of religious and non-religious worldviews.

View 2: knowledge and understanding as personal interpretation

In contrast to this emphasis on objectivity is the view of understanding inspired by the work of, amongst others, the philosopher Hans-Georg Gadamer.[5] His argument is that any attempt at understanding an event always begins in what he calls a pre-understanding. In other words, no one is a blank slate; as humans, we approach new knowledge with certain assumptions that will influence how we understand that knowledge. To understand anything, we all start from somewhere. We all make interpretations of the knowledge we gain based on our predilections. In other words, we all inhabit a personal worldview that predisposes us to understand and interpret events and experiences in particular ways.

A story may help in explaining this alternative view.

Major Charles Ingram became famous in 2001 for his criminal conviction for cheating on the Quiz show *Who Wants to be a Millionaire*? (Incidentally he continues to protest his innocence.) The cheating was alleged to be that Ingram's wife and another audience member were coughing at strategic points in the show to indicate correct answers.

In the TV drama *Quiz* about this incident, aired in April 2020, there is a courtroom scene where the defence and prosecution barristers argue about the facts of the case. The prosecution claims that the facts are that there were 19 coughs at key points in the show. To prove their case they relied on an edited video tape of the show made by the production company that was claiming to have been cheated. This had been edited to enhance the offending coughing so as to highlight the asserted objective facts surrounding these 19 significant coughs.

In response, the defence barrister made the following assertion: "All memories are a lie". This wasn't meant literally. Her point was that memories are always an interpretation of the facts as to what actually happened, edited by the brain to reflect the story believed in by the storyteller. She then went on to criticise the prosecution video on the basis that it was not a presentation of the brute (objective) facts, but rather a presentation of the production company's *interpretation* of those facts. She pointed out that the video editor deliberately selected 19 of the total 192 audience coughs that occurred during the show and then enhanced those 19 coughs to make them clearly audible when they were not so on the day of the crime. The defence barrister's intention was to persuade the jury that they were not just viewing brute facts when watching the prosecution video, but were rather being immersed in the production company's interpretation of events edited in the light of their belief that Charles Ingram had attempted to defraud them of one million pounds. And her job was to convince the jury to side with the Ingram's understanding of the events. Unfortunately for her and the Ingrams, the jury were not so persuaded. The dispute goes on through the appeals process.

This story illustrates the fundamental importance of interpretation in human knowledge and the importance of learning to make good judgements when assessing different interpretations of events. To do this well is to become an educated meaning-maker; that is a lifelong enterprise.

Understanding in RE?

The critical question is how these differences in understanding of understanding are dealt with in RE? Are pupils educated about the role that pre-understanding and interpretation play in how we as humans understand knowledge, or are they simply told what the *objective* understanding of the facts is? Are they introduced to the challenging business of interpretation and helped to make judgements for themselves? Or are they simply given information to master?

Gadamer's suggestion is that to gain informed understanding there needs to be a dialogic process. This entails the learner approaching the facts from their personal worldview, but being open to that being challenged by other worldviews that may offer different interpretations. The implication of Gadamer's understanding of understanding is that it does not come through mastery of objective facts, but rather it comes through dialogue with worldviews that are different from one's own. It entails relational interaction between teacher, student and object of study. The concept of mastery of knowledge is replaced by the concept of *personal dialogue with knowledge*.[6] As we will see, this dramatically changes the pedagogy.

However, before considering that, we need to consider the implication these different views of understanding have for the important aspiration that RE should be *objective*. If you operate with the first view of understanding, then being objective means adopting a neutral, non-biased, descriptive approach to teaching and learning. In this framing, a teacher who teaches objectively teaches established facts. An objective pupil is meant to focus on these facts with a view to recalling them in the future.

However, adopting the second view of understanding entails a very different approach. Here being objective is being reflexive; it is being able to identify one's own pre-understandings and those of others; it is to learn to represent the lived experience of others as best you can, but acknowledging that you can never be neutral. Here understanding is about both the subject matter and yourself and the dialogue that happens between the two. Such understanding is relational, taking seriously the role of personal interpretation in the growth of knowledge.

The CoRE Report states that the purpose of RE is "understanding the human quest for meaning, being prepared for life in a diverse world and having space to reflect on one's own worldview."[7] This purpose clearly resonates with the second view of understanding, because that emphasises the promotion of personal reflection on one's own personal worldview and a dialogic (rather than mastery) encounter with the subject matter of organised worldviews. The danger with the first view of understanding is how it treats pupils, reducing them to containers into which knowledge is poured (or brains on sticks as James K.A. Smith provocatively suggests) rather than treating them as persons who can interact with and be changed by the experience of learning.

Implications for pedagogy: the importance of hermeneutics

> Two young fish were swimming in the sea when a respected elder fish swam towards them. As he passed he shared a greeting. "How's the water today lads?" A few moments after the encounter, one of the younger fish turned to the other. "What the heck is water?"

Michael Grimmitt was a key influence in the development of modern RE.[8] He was troubled by the idea of curriculum as "a commodity which the government could deliver to teachers in schools who subsequently would *implement and deliver* it to pupils".[9] His vision was that pupils "should evaluate their understanding of religion in personal terms and evaluate their understanding of self in religious terms".[10] For Grimmitt, pedagogy is all about promoting an educational interaction between the pupils and the subject content they are studying. The teacher's professional responsibility lies in the design of this interaction. His thinking here reflects Gadamer's view of understanding.

A very important claim in the CoRE Report is: "It is one of the core tasks of education to enable each pupil to understand, reflect on and develop their own personal worldview".[11] This clearly resonates with Grimmitt's approach to pedagogy. In terms of our three fish above, the role of the teacher is to behave like the elder fish who wishes to challenge the two younger fish to reflect on their own taken-for-granted view of the world and the taken-for-granted view of the world embedded in the content they are learning about. Such an approach highlights the importance of the pupils' personal processing of what they learn alongside the faithful representation of the worldview tradition being studied. The nature of the interaction between these two dimensions is fundamental to good pedagogy. CoRE, however, is silent on how this might happen – understandably as it was not a report on classroom pedagogy.

Central to my argument is the proposal that Religion and Worldviews teaching will need to adopt a hermeneutical approach if it is to do justice to CoRE's aspired shift to worldview. Hermeneutics is "the theory that everything is a matter of interpretation".[12] It is the recognition that we cannot occupy a worldview-free position of pure reason. A hermeneutical pedagogy is based on the belief that pupils should be taught how to function well in a world pervaded by interpretation. By adopting a hermeneutical approach, RE can take forward CoRE's aspiration that pupils will "understand, reflect on and develop their own personal worldview".

Here I will draw on the work of the theologian Anthony Thiselton, who was particularly interested in the interpretation of biblical texts. He coined the phrase "responsible hermeneutics", which focuses both teachers' and pupils' attention on "exactly what are we doing when we read, understand and apply texts?"[13] Generalised, this question becomes: what exactly is going on when a pupil encounters different worldviews in the classroom?

The implication of Thiselton's argument is that every teacher and pupil should be aware that they approach the knowledge to be learnt with a "pre-understanding", which he describes as "an initial and provisional stage in the journey towards understanding something more fully".[14] This is echoing the widely accepted hermeneutical insight that every pupil and teacher approaches the text from the vantage point of their own worldview (sometimes called the reader's horizon). It is therefore essential to be reflexive about one's own pre-understanding and the impact of that on one's reception of another person's worldview. This applies to both pupil and teacher.[15]

Some may worry this is an overly subjective view of knowledge. However, Thiselton is clear that a text cannot be made to mean just anything. There are legitimate interpretations and others that are plainly just wrong if care is taken in reading the text. It is the same when learning about a worldview in RE. Some interpretations are plainly wrong. Taking care to avoid these is very important. Others are disputable, although they may also be tenable. Pupils have to learn to make justifiable interpretations and not just assume that all that matters is having an opinion. That is what Thiselton means by responsible hermeneutics.

Richard Kueh, the RE subject lead for Ofsted, recently outlined three types of knowledge that teachers should incorporate in academically robust RE.[16] The first he called the substantive content, which I suggest will largely consist of information about and concepts from organised worldviews. This has been the main focus of the world religions approach. The second he calls disciplinary knowledge, by which he means the way(s) of knowing, such as theology and philosophy, that will be used by the pupils in their learning of the substantive content. The third he calls personal knowledge, where pupils learn more about their own personal worldview. This is where spiritual development happens. The interaction of these three types of knowledge is a hermeneutical process where awareness of worldview is developed by the pupils. In this way, the study of Religion and Worldviews will contribute to their academic understanding, their personal development and their growth as active citizens.

Practical examples

That all sounds very abstract. What might this actually look like in a classroom? For the rest of this chapter we will explore four relatively recent examples of published resources that help in starting to answer this question. None of them is the definitive worldview approach – but they all illustrate what an approach based on a worldview paradigm might begin to look like, from the perspective of different disciplines.

a.   Who is Jesus? A Religious Studies approach

By a religious studies approach I mean the explicit study of religions. We begin with what colloquially might be referred to as a "bog-standard" topic for school RE: *Who is Jesus*? On first glance it might seem obvious what needs to be taught here. Pupils surely need to learn about Jesus' birth, his parables, the Sermon on the Mount, his crucifixion, the Christian belief that he was the Son of God and the claims concerning his miracles and resurrection. Once they know these things, then they will understand who Jesus "is". The focus is on pupils learning facts, namely what the Bible tells us about Jesus. The assumption of such an approach is clear: if pupils know the stories in the gospels, then they will understand who Jesus is.

In 2018, a resource for upper secondary schools entitled *Who is Jesus*? appeared that took a very different approach to this topic.[17] It shows how the worldview paradigm makes RE a very different experience. Opening the contents page is an immediate revelation. Chapters include:

— Who is Jesus for gospel writers?

— Who is Jesus for Muslims?

— Who is Jesus for feminists?

— Who is Jesus for Christians today?

The resource works by introducing pupils to different disciplines such as Biblical studies, Islamic theology and Christian contextual theology, through the eyes of different academics who appear regularly through the resource making comments and explaining ideas. Each chapter concludes with questions for the pupils. Examples from the Muslim chapter are:

— What are the similarities and differences in Muslim and Christian views about Jesus' nature?

— Why might Christians not be satisfied with the Muslim view of Jesus as a prophet?

— Why might Muslims argue against the belief that Jesus is the Son of God?

The key thing to note is that this resource introduces pupils to interpretation and perspective. They still have to know the stories from the gospels, but what they learn is that people interpret those stories from the perspective of their own worldview. Furthermore, they learn that we each have to make judgments about the validity of each other's interpretations on the basis of evidence. This is a clear example of a hermeneutical approach. Pupils learn that there is no worldview-free answer to the question "Who is Jesus?". To answer it for yourself you have to weigh what different people say against the evidence that is available to you. That's what we call research.

The missing element in this resource is that, in its focus on understanding other people's perspectives, it doesn't give enough space to seeing how the pupil's personal worldview understanding might be developed. The main focus is on understanding how people who speak for organised worldviews respond to the Jesus question. In that sense it hasn't fully moved on from the world religions paradigm. There are two chapters that look at how individuals do interpret Jesus based on their own life experience. One is an artist and one a professor of RE who went blind in mid-career and wrote extensively on his reactions to that experience as a Christian. But there probably isn't enough attention to helping the pupils themselves reflect on their own response to Jesus as part of their personal worldview development.

b.   Metacognition and worldviews: a philosophical approach

By a philosophical approach I mean here one that focuses on the question of how we come to know things. In this case study, this question is pursued through a sustained emphasis on the pupils' understanding of their own personal worldview development. The publication in question is entitled *Metacognition, Worldviews and Religious Education*.[18] Though not an immediately compelling title, this book was developed in close cooperation with primary school teachers. It is therefore a good complement to the *Who is Jesus?* resource that was designed for upper secondary pupils and which may have led some readers to think that the worldview paradigm only works for secondary. Instead of focusing on a particular curriculum topic, this resource provides a model for a way of working that exemplifies the worldview paradigm. It does this by creating three zones in the classroom:

— Meta-thinking zone – thinking about thinking and learning in RE (thinking processes)

— Worldview zone – thinking about myself as a learner in RE (self-awareness)

— Resources zone – thinking about representations of (non-)religious phenomena in RE (encounter with subject knowledge)[19]

Moving between these zones illustrates how pupils can be helped with their own personal worldview development by focusing on their own thinking and learning. One teacher describes a year 5 lesson on Hinduism where prompts like "what do I – know, think, remember, guess and believe?" were used to inform group discussion.[20] The rationale is given as:

> If RE is conceptualised as a journey in which pupils move from peripheral to full participation in the ongoing dialogues of communities of academic inquiry concerned with the study of religion(s) and worldview(s), then as part of that journey they need to develop ever greater awareness of themselves as learners, meaning-makers and knowledge-producers.[21]

As part of their work in the worldview zone, pupils are asked over time to develop a "worldview profile" or reflective diary that enables them to become aware of and develop their own positioning as a key element in becoming a self-reflexive learner. The authors state:

> Worldview consciousness enables pupils to understand their own interpretation of, and engagement with, curriculum content

and to engage more deeply and in more genuine dialogue with the opinions of others.[22]

The authors are frank in their assessment that this approach needs further work to ensure that pupil responses are not shallow, but the sophisticated theoretical foundation and practical exemplification by teachers offers an early example of the new paradigm. It is clearly an explicit focus on reflection on the pre-understanding that pupils' bring to their encounter with the subject content in a dialogical approach.

Unfortunately, by highlighting one zone as the worldview zone, the impression could be given that the other two zones are not part of the worldview approach. That is not the case. In zones 1 and 3 pupils are focusing on important dimensions of a worldview approach by learning about how their thinking works and by learning how to represent organised worldviews well. It might have helped if zone 2 was called the *personal* worldview zone.

c. Big Ideas: a sociological approach

By a sociological approach, I here mean a focus on understanding human behaviour in community. If RE teachers are asked to name the Big Ideas in their subject, they will often respond with concepts like Incarnation (Christianity) or Ummah (Islam), Torah (Judaism) or Secularism (Humanism). These are, of course, quite correct as they embody some of the key concepts that characterise these particular organised worldviews. One would certainly expect them to be taught in RE. But this response from teachers indicates the current dominance of the world religions paradigm. An alternative approach is offered by Barbara Wintersgill, who offers six that focus on understanding how human worldviews develop.[23] They are:

1. Continuity, Change and Diversity
2. Words and Beyond
3. A Good Life
4. Making Sense of Life's Experiences
5. Influence and Power
6. The Big Picture

These six ideas are an attempt to capture the disciplinary knowledge that pupils need to acquire in order to develop a rigorous academic understanding of the place that religious and non-religious worldviews play in human life. For example, to grasp Big Idea 5 is to develop an understanding of how particular religious and non-religious communities gain influence in society at large. This might entail a study of an established religion like the Church of England, contrasting it with the Free Church movement. Or it might involve a study of Rowan Williams' idea of procedural and programmatic secularisms, perhaps using the case of India's transition from Ghandi's secular state to Modi's BJP Hindu state.[24] These may sound like difficult topics for schools, but they are no more challenging to teach than big ideas like Incarnation, which teachers have been used to handling from key stage 1 for many years. Perhaps a more familiar example would be to examine the changing place of festivals like Christmas, Diwali and Eid in British life over the years. At key stage 1, Wintersgill suggests that a key question to focus on with pupils when looking at this Big Idea might be "are religions important anymore?"

The Big Ideas approach is very different from that which many teachers are used to. It is like the National Entitlement in the CoRE report in that it lays out the knowledge and understanding that pupils need to develop in order to understand how worldviews operate in human life. It does not specify the actual examples of religious and non-religious material to be taught (substantive content); that decision is left to the teacher, although ideas are offered in supplementary publications. Neither is it hermeneutical in approach as it does not directly address the pupil's interaction with the substantive content. It is however a very helpful approach in identifying the questions that are central to understanding how worldviews function in human life.

d. Understanding Christianity: a theological approach

By a theological approach, I mean one that utilises the thinking of religious people. For example, *Understanding Christianity* is an initiative of the Church of England, developed in response to inspection reports (both its own and from Ofsted), that highlighted pupils' poor understanding of Christian beliefs.[25] Its focus is on pupils coming to understand Christianity as a living world faith through exploring eight core theological concepts, for example God, Incarnation and the Kingdom of God. It offers a spiral, developmental approach whereby children encounter the eight concepts in more academically demanding forms as they progress through their years of schooling.

So far, this is not particularly new and could be seen as just a doctrinal version of the world religions paradigm. But *Understanding Christianity*'s distinctive contribution lies in its translating of the ideas of hermeneutical theologians Anthony Thiselton and Kevin Vanhoozer into forms that teachers can use from early years through to key stage 4. It does this through its pedagogy that highlights three elements:

— **Making Sense of the Text** is where pupils learn how to read and interpret Bible passages by paying close attention to the texts and their meanings for Christians. This is where pupils learn to listen carefully to

Christianity, to represent the understanding of Christians concerning their faith and to develop their own skills of interpretation.

— **Understanding the Impact** is where pupils examine different ways in which Christians put their beliefs that they derive from their texts into action, as individuals and in community. Pupils learn how texts are interpreted differently when people inhabit different contexts. They come to understand that there are a number of Christian worldviews, not just one. They also consider how Christian worldviews over centuries have influenced contemporary thinking and living.

— **Making Connections** is where pupils learn how to make connections between the texts they meet, the eight core concepts and their wider learning. It is also where they reflect on and discern possible connections between their personal worldview and the Christian worldviews they have learnt about.

Through this approach, pupils are encouraged to reflect on their own response to the major threads in the 'big story' of the Bible. However, given its focus on doctrinal themes, it seems the hermeneutical emphasis is more on understanding the teachings of Christianity than on the pupils' reflexive response. It is more focused on the organised worldview of Christianity than the personal worldview of the pupil, although it does include examination of different Christian personal worldview responses to the doctrinal themes.

Conclusion

This brief survey of four recent pedagogical approaches illustrates how the worldview paradigm is distinctively different from the world religions paradigm. It offers a greater emphasis both on understanding the process of interpretation, and on the development of the pupil's personal worldview, through the dialogic encounter with organised worldviews in classrooms. Our survey also illustrates how varied the implementation approaches to the worldview paradigm can be. No doubt advocates of these different approaches will be quite critical of each other! The worldview paradigm will not create a one-size-fits-all model for RE. Rather, what is sought is a variety of approaches that put learning to be accurate, critical, wise and reflexive interpreters at its heart. This is achieved by emphasising the academic rigour of multi-disciplinary learning about organised worldviews in a way that promotes reflection on people's personal worldviews, both the adherents learnt about and the pupils themselves. However, it is early days yet. I anticipate that syllabuses and resources that seek to fulfil the vision of the new paradigm will continue to appear over the coming years. The RE Council is currently seeking to support such initiatives by sponsoring projects that clarify the key features of the paradigm and by developing further exemplification material that will support syllabus writers.

1 See Trevor Cooling, Doing God in Education (London: Theos, 2010), pp27-37 and Trevor Cooling, *A Christian Vision for State Education* (London: SPCK Publishing, 1994) Ch. 6 for a fuller discussion of the issues discussed in this section.

2 This is of course an oversimplification of a complex issue. But the core message that there is a choice to be made is defensible.

3 Kate Christopher, 'Don't panic, it's just change: a single educational rationale aim for Religion and Worldviews' in Mark Chater (ed.) *Reforming Religious Education: Power and Knowledge in a Worldviews Curriculum* (Woodbridge: John Catt, 2020), pp. 83-90.

4 See Kate Christopher, 'Don't panic...' p. 89; Trevor Cooling, Doing God.., Ch. 1. and Trevor Cooling, Beth Green, Andrew Morris and Lynn Revell, *Christian Faith in English Church Schools: Research Conversations with Classroom Teachers* (Oxford: Peter Lang, 2016), pp. 144-145.

5 For a full discussion of the potential relevance of Gadamer's philosophy in RE see David Aldridge, 'Religious education's double hermeneutic', *British Journal of RE* 40:3 (2018), pp. 245-256.

6 Parker J Palmer's *To Know as We are Known: Education As A Spiritual Journey* (San Francisco: Harper, 1983) is a classic statement of this view of understanding.

7 CoRE, *Religion and...* p73.

8 Michael Grimmitt, *Religious Education and...*

9 Michael Grimmitt, *Pedagogies of Religious Education* (Great Wakering: McCrimmons, 2000), p. 8.

10 Michael Grimmitt, *Pedagogies...* p. 15. This was written before it was widely accepted that non-religious worldviews should be included in RE.

11 CoRE, *Religion and...* p.5.

12 John Caputo, *Hermeneutics: Facts and Interpretation in the Age of Information* (London: Pelican, 2018), p. 4.

13 Anthony Thiselton, *Hermeneutics: An Introduction* (London: SPCK, 2009), p. 4.

14 Thiselton, Hermeneutics... p. 12.

15 See Ruth Flanagan, 'Implementing a Ricoeurian lens to examine the impact of individuals' worldviews on subject content knowledge in RE in England: a theoretical proposition', *British Journal of Religious Education* published online (9th October 2019) for recent research on teacher training students.

16 Ofsted is the school inspection agency for England. These points were made in the plenary presented at the RExChange conference organised by Culham St

Gabriel's Trust on 3rd October 2020. See *https://www.cstg.org.uk/programmes/rexchange/*

17 Rob Freathy et al., *Who is Jesus?* (Exeter: Exeter University, 2018).

18 Shirley Larkin et al., *Metacognition, Worldviews and Religious Education: A Practical Guide for Teachers* (London: Routledge, 2019).

19 Larkin et al., *Metacognition...* p. 10.

20 Larkin et al., *Metacognition...* p. 39.

21 Larkin et al., *Metacognition...* p. 43.

22 Larkin et al., *Metacognition...* p. 115.

23 Barbara Wintersgill, *Putting Big Ideas into Practice in Religious Education* (2019). *www.reonline.org.uk/resources/putting-big-ideas-into-practice-in-religious-education*

23 These are one selection of Big Ideas. Rob Freathy and Helen John have offered an alternative to this selection in 'Worldviews and Big Ideas...'

24 Rowan Williams, *Faith in the Public Square*, (London: Bloomsbury, 2012).

25 Stephen Pett (ed), *Understanding Christianity: Text, Impact, Connections* (Birmingham: Christian Education Publications, 2016). *www.understandingchristianity.org.uk*

26 Stephen Pett and Trevor Cooling, 'Understanding Christianity: exploring a hermeneutical pedagogy for teaching Christianity', *British Journal of Religious Education* 40:3, (2018), pp. 257-267.

4
Religious influence in and on Religious Education

In this penultimate chapter, we turn to the question of the place of religious commitment in this new worldview paradigm. I examine and reject the argument that representatives of religious worldviews should not have influence in RE. Rather I argue for the recognition that everyone involved in RE influences the subject from the perspective of their personal worldview. The critical question is, I suggest, what makes this responsible influence? Finally, I examine three examples of what might be regarded as responsible religious influence.

As we have seen in Chapter 2, some people have expressed concern about the potential dilution of the subject in the worldview paradigm, with religion ceasing to be a central focus. In contrast, others are calling for the subject to be just about worldviews, with religion having no special attention. That was clearly not the intention of CoRE, because the title they recommended for the subject was "*Religion* and Worldviews". But, given this acceptance of a central focus for religion, what influence should religious people have on how it is taught?

The concern about religious influence

There are significant voices that view religious influence in RE as unwelcome (both in giving religion significant attention in the subject content and in the power that religious communities have to influence the curriculum) and who call for "a *wholly* educational rationale" for teaching about worldviews.[1] Its legitimate aspiration is that education should be inclusive, designed to meet the *educational* needs of *all* pupils, irrespective of their own background or personal worldview. It should seek to support the development of critical, autonomous and wise judgment on the part of pupils.

However, a worrying interpretation of how that can be achieved is to propose that institutional religious communities should be excluded from having shaping influence in schools, and certainly not on the curriculum.[2] The aspiration appears to be that there is a neutral or objective or rationally-settled position, what is sometimes called view from nowhere, upon which a wholly educational approach can be based such that pupils are able freely to make their own worldview decisions.[3]

As already indicated, there are two issues that get muddled together in this debate about religious influence. The first relates to the presence of religious character schools in the government-funded public education system.[4] The second relates to the influence of religious bodies on the nature and practice of RE in all schools through their membership of committees that approve syllabuses, their influence on government and their capacity to produce widely-used resources like *Understanding Christianity*.[5] The two merge because it is the presence of religious character schools in the education system that gives religious organisations influence in discussions of RE, particularly with government.

A recent tract from the Philosophy of Education Society of Great Britain illustrates the position taken by the critics of religious influence.[6] Entitled *How to regulate faith schools*, it records the main conclusions of a project based at Warwick University that reviewed policy towards religious-ethos schooling from a philosophical standpoint. The report correctly highlights some very important questions about the civic responsibilities of schools to wider society in raising democratic citizens who contribute to the common good. It also, rightly, stresses the importance of pupils learning about and experiencing religions and cultures different from their

own so that they are not simply entrapped in their parents'
cultural or religious preferences.

The tract's central premise is that the risks to children's
autonomy from a religiously-shaped education outweigh
parental rights to choose the educational culture they favour
for their children. This concern for autonomy is legitimate,
but a particular view of autonomy is uncritically adopted. It
is argued that it is illegitimate for schools to act "with the
intention that they should endorse any particular view about
how to live their lives" or to include practices that "form
children's developing identities and create deep attachments".[7]
Critically, the assumption appears to be that these risks to
autonomy exist *only* in so-called faith schools where there
is religious influence. There is no discussion of this risk in
schools that do not have a religious character. The assumption
appears to be made that it is possible to create a non-shaping
school ethos in these. "Faith" schools are assumed to be
fundamentally different from other schools in this respect.

Picking on "faith" schools in this way because they are
deemed to be directive, whilst assuming the non-directive
nature of non-faith (sic) schools, ignores all the insights of the
worldview discussion that has been so influential in the last
fifty years.[8] It rests on the view of understanding as rational
objectivity critiqued in Chapter 3. But that is incompatible
with the notion of worldview. The alternative literature
arguing that *all* education is influenced by particular forms of
worldview is not mentioned in the tract.[9] This narrow selection
is astonishing in what purports to be a comprehensive review
of the philosophical discussions of policy on faith schools.
The question of whether non-faith schools are implicated
in the transmission of worldview is simply not addressed.
As research with student teachers has found, it is far too

easy to assume that because you are non-religious, you do not have a worldview and are not therefore at risk of being inappropriately directive as an educator.[10]

For now, I will assume that worldview is always a shaping influence in education, whatever the school, be it of religious character or not. Then "understanding" is as an act of interpretation that always begins from a pre-understanding. Given this, the question then becomes: how can the inevitable worldview influence that all schools and all teachers exert be exercised in a responsible and professional way that promotes both the autonomy and the critical judgement of the pupils? We will pursue this question through three practical examples taken from research projects undertaken by the National Institute for Christian Education Research.[11]

An approach to GCSE RE[12]

The case study that follows is from a year-long research project working with 14 teachers in three English church secondary schools, exploring how they understood the influence of the school's Christian ethos on their classroom work.[13] The research used a method called *What If Learning* to prompt reflection by the teachers. This draws teachers' attention to the pre-understandings that are present in the classroom.

Angela was Head of Religious Education in a secondary school. Her school was proud of her achievements, particularly highlighting the fact that Ofsted had filmed her for a best practice video.[14] She achieved excellent GCSE results and the school considered this to be a very important expression of its Church ethos.[15]

For the research project, Angela worked on a GCSE Christian ethics lesson focusing on the question of assisted dying. Her usual approach had been for her teaching to follow the pattern of the exam questions. This entailed the pupils marshalling three arguments for and three arguments against assisted dying, with the pupils finally offering their own opinion. The three arguments for were taken from secular sources to do with human rights and the three arguments against came from the Christian Bible and were based on the sanctity of life.

Angela found involvement in the research process really upsetting because it revealed certain hidden assumptions embedded in her pedagogy. It dawned on her that she was allowing the worldview assumed by the exam board to frame the way she taught, rather than the worldview underpinning the school's Christian ethos. In particular, she realised that her pupils were learning that Christian ethics is largely about winning arguments, that Christians do this by marshalling Bible verses as proof texts, and that the conflict is binary (truth is on one side, error is on the other) from this exam board approach. "Christians against the Secularists" was the underlying message. The assumption was that to be a faithful Christian in an ethical dispute entails trying to win the argument. None of these things were actually said to the pupils; they were rather embedded in the exam-inspired pedagogy. This was the unexamined transmission of an unquestioned worldview perspective shaped by a secular education institution, namely the exam board.

As part of the research Angela did her own theological reading, which convinced her that a more faithful representation of Christian ethics was to focus on the idea of being hospitable.[16] The first response in an ethical debate should not then be an attempt to win an argument, but an attempt to understand one's apparent opponent. This radically changed her approach to teaching. She abandoned her "for and against" approach and instead designed a narrative lesson based on the life and death of Tony Nicklinson who was a campaigner for assisted dying, having been left in a locked-in state after a massive stroke in his fifties. The pupils were set tasks where they had to explain why Nicklinson felt the way he did and what the anxieties were of the pro-life campaigners who blocked the legislation change that he wanted to secure. This pedagogical shift changed the worldview messaging of the course from Christian ethics being about winning arguments based on assumed Christian absolutes, to Christian ethics being learning to understand people's positions on very challenging issues and to listen carefully before leaping into adopting a position.

You may not agree with Angela's shift, but that is not the point here. What matters is that her experience in this project highlights how RE classroom teaching is framed by often undeclared positions that the pupils may not be aware of and could well be controversial, but which are highly influential in the development of pupils' understanding. Angela's epiphany in this project was to become aware of this fact. The point is that teachers in their classrooms and schools as a whole cannot avoid shaping the pupils' experience from a worldview perspective. There is no possibility of a worldview-neutral approach. All education is a process of formation. The important question is this: is that influence undertaken responsibly?[17] It will not be if only some teachers and some

All education is a process of formation.

schools, those of religious character, are considered to be at risk of inappropriate influence. To be responsible influence, the pupils must be alerted to the worldview assumptions that pervade their educational experience. In Angela's case this was done by a) becoming aware of the worldview perspective she was working with, b) choosing one that was academically more credible and c) discussing that with her pupils.

Christian Physical Education (PE)?

The next example is of what responsible worldview influence might look like in areas of the curriculum other than RE. No doubt the notion of Christian Physical Education sounds odd to many readers. To explain this, I will share an example of a teacher coaching a class of twelve-year-old boys in a hockey class in what he believed was a distinctively Christian but responsible manner. This comes from the previously mentioned research on teachers in English church secondary schools.[18]

As a male PE teacher, James was very concerned about the unexamined influence of elite sport on his pupils' character development. In particular, he was concerned about the admiration it created for celebrity and wealth and how it focused attention on an individual's status. He wanted to offer a different aspiration. So instead of PE in the school being framed by the unexamined valuing of elite individual performance, he decided to reframe it with the notion of valuing learning to be a sports coach. The clue to what happened in the lesson we observed came from the subsequent pupil focus group when they were asked what they thought they were doing in the lesson. They told us, "we were learning how to encourage each other".

The lesson commenced with a standard demonstration of the basic "push pass"; the position of feet, the position of ball, the position of hands, the movement of stick, and so forth. Then the pupils were divided into pairs and were tasked with coaching each other. They were required to score and report back on how their partner performed. However, the focal task was for each of them to identify how they encouraged their partner. This was then discussed in a group activity at the end of the lesson.

How then is this responsible *Christian* influence? First, it is Christian influence. The reframing of the approach was because James drew, in the way that he taught, on his Christian worldview by his valuing of encouraging behaviour that he adopted to challenge the pervasive influence of society's valuing of elite performance. Of course, that is not a *uniquely* Christian thing to value, but for James it was a *distinctive* aspect of his Christian worldview. Second, it was responsible influence because he did not hijack the PE curriculum to teach theology. Rather, he framed the current PE curriculum in a different way. Furthermore, he made the pupils aware of what he had done by discussing the notions of elite sport performance and encouraging coaching behavior with them. They were thereby sensitised to the influence of that worldview, and set free to make their own reflexive choices in the years to come. Openness and reflexivity about the inevitable influence of worldview was what made this responsible influence.

Sacred texts, teachers and worldview education

The third example addresses the question "how should sacred texts such as the Bible and the Qur'an feature in classrooms and the curriculum?" Should these be taught in some 'objective' fashion or should teaching be shaped in any way by the religious community for which they are sacred? Many people would regard this as confessional and therefore, inappropriate. In the section that follows, Bob Bowie discusses research around the possibilities for a hermeneutical approach in school. By hermeneutics is meant the study of how religious people read their sacred texts and not just the study of the content of those texts. Bob's research points to teaching approaches that are drawn from the work of sacred text scholars from within faith communities. It is offered as an exemplar of appropriate religious influence in school RE. I hand over to Bob now to explain this work.

Research shows that poor text use is a significant problem in RE.[19] Too often studying sacred texts is reduced to the memorisation of quotes. Learning about the interpretation of texts takes second place to learning preconceived associations between certain texts and certain issues. Secondary school exams encourage proof-text debates, where students look for Bible verses to support particular positions on contentious issues. Quotations are put into categories of, for example, 'for war' and 'against war', and pupils are asked to debate how it is possible that some Christians become pacifists while some think wars can be just. Pupils might learn that religion is full of arguments and people have opposing points of view supported with quotes from sacred texts.[20]

However, the scholarship of the discipline of sacred texts study within the religious community is not prominent. The vast majority of pupils do not study a book of the Bible in entirety. They are not asked to explain how a Christian goes about engaging with the Bible or how scholars go about investigating it. The ways people find different kinds of meaning in texts, such as through worship, prayer, meditation and personal reflection, slip out of view as lessons become primarily focused on binary-issue debates with single answers. These things matter, because the way teachers handle texts in the classroom shapes pupils' classroom experience, and therefore their understanding, of these texts.

The Italian philosopher Umberto Eco argued that there was a skill in being a model or good reader, which was to become proficient in handling the text in the ways it was first handled by its authors, hearers and audiences. We can add to that the ways communities who continue to hold those texts dear handle them today in literal, moral, spiritual and symbolic ways.[21]

But how to do this in the classroom? Texts and Teachers was a research project led by me with Farid Panjwani and Katie Clemmey.[22] The project sought to address this challenge of teaching sacred texts by offering teachers the opportunity to experiment with hermeneutical approaches that helped pupils to engage with the task of interpretation as practiced in sacred text scholarship in Christianity and Islam.

The project team worked with ten teachers in seven diverse schools for a year (Catholic, Ecumenical, Church of England and non-religious). The schools were very different in character, kind and pupil composition. Modest professional development support was provided, and teachers were encouraged to experiment in their curricula. The results were fascinating.

The teachers who taught their curricula more hermeneutically saw benefits for their pupils and felt encouraged to expand this approach. They engaged with longer extracts of texts and found a positive pupil response to this. They developed the tools of text analysis in key stage 3, which they found helpful preparation for GCSE. They reported examples of a different quality of dialogue in their lessons, where pupils explored the multiple dimensions of meaning around text (spiritual, symbolic, moral, literal, etc.). Participants found students could progress from the study of sacred text in one tradition to another, and that the study in the classroom in some cases triggered reflections on personal worldview.

One participant teacher recalled a conversation with a sixth form student who had achieved a very high grade in GCSE Religious Studies. In the sixth form general RE, where the participant was running the hermeneutics course, it became clear that this particular student had no understanding of what symbolic meaning meant. That you could excel at the highest level at GCSE in this subject, without a conception of symbolism and metaphor, points to an absent building block that should be at the heart of the subject.

Texts and Teachers was a secondary school focused project but sacred text educators think hermeneutics is a primary school issue as well. Dr. Margaret Carswell works with primary children and teachers in Australia and the UK, using a range of practical techniques to enable young children to get some sense of the different hermeneutical dimensions critical in sacred text scholarship.[23] For instance, she suggests classroom teachers can use an empty chair when exploring a Gospel story in the Bible, to remind very young children that there is a human author of this text who we cannot see in the words. She uses the example of reading a newspaper to demonstrate how we learn to navigate different kinds of literary forms within a single collection of texts (agony aunt letters, sports reports, the editorial and the front page). This helps pupils to understand the difference between, for instance, psalms, letters, parables, gospels and histories and how some of these find their way into hymns and worship music, others into teachings on moral matters, and how others still may shape the organisation of a religious community.

Pupils can develop practices for investigating sacred texts and how texts are engaged within religious traditions and the lives of people of different worldviews. *Texts and Teachers* found that the way teachers framed the sacred texts in their language, their questions, and their curriculum design mattered. Teachers could introduce pupils to the world of the sacred text scholar, even exploring sophisticated and challenging questions such as whether meaning depends on there being a reader, and how we can reliably judge differing or contrasting interpretations. The teachers spoke powerfully about the way this scholarly approach seemed to open a door for the pupils and often led to a kind of classroom conversation the teachers had not experienced before. They gave rich examples of interactions between the pupils' personal worldviews and the approaches to reading sacred texts that they studied in the classroom.

Taking a more hermeneutical approach matters for many reasons. First, there is the ambition that pupils should encounter disciplinary knowledge as well as lists of facts and figures; Sacred Text Scholarship offers disciplinary knowledge. Second, there is the ambition that students learn about the different ways traditions, communities and individuals find and make meaning; this is the *nuts and bolts* of hermeneutics. Third, there is the civic contribution that pupils are introduced to a critical eye on the use and sometimes abuse of texts especially, but not only, sacred ones. Finally, there is the goal of examining how sacred texts are read throughout life by people as they face new and different challenges. Most importantly here, it illustrates how religious commitment can be a responsible influence in RE by providing an academically rigorous model for approaching sacred texts.

Conclusion

The legitimate question concerning religious or other worldview influence is then "will that inevitable influence be exercised irresponsibly?" and not "how can we avoid any influence?" The point is that the risk of being an inappropriate influencer exists for all educators and all schools, not just the religious. The challenge is to develop an ethical approach to this fact of life that all educators can adopt.[24] This approach will need to be based on the interpretive view of understanding in educational contexts that I described in Chapter 3, which highlights the importance of reflexivity and openness with respect to worldview influence and assumptions. It will mean all schools and teachers being open as to the hidden assumptions which the school takes for granted in its structures, curriculum and vision and allowing pupils the space to explore challenges to them.

> The legitimate question concerning religious or other worldview influence is then "will that inevitable influence be exercised irresponsibly?" and not "how can we avoid any influence?"

As we saw in Chapter 2, much of the fear of religious influence is based in the expectation that it will be totalising, in other words making "ideological power grabs" for pupils' minds and hearts.[25] Unfortunately, sometimes it is. The offenders, however, will not just be religious character schools, but any school that seeks to impose an unexamined worldview on its pupils. That may be a religious character school, if its sole aim is to make the pupils into believers in the mold of that particular institution. Or it may be a non-religious school that, for example, seeks to mold its pupils into the unquestioned assumption that success in life is defined by elite performance. The Church of England is one example of a religious institution seeking to exercise responsible influence. Its stated vision, *Deeply Christian, Serving the Common Good*, attempts to define the character of an inclusive education based on a Christian worldview that is appropriate for pupils from a range of religious and non-religious backgrounds.[26] It would be heartening to see all schools attempting such vision statements.

1   See for example Mark Chater's and Alan Brine's contributions to *Reforming RE...* (Emphasis is mine).

2   For example, Humanists UK has a long-running campaign against "faith school discrimination". See *humanism.org.uk/2020/01/21/inclusive-education-for-all-an-interview-with-humanists-uk-education-campaigns-manager-dr-ruth-wareham/*

3   See Cooling, *Doing God...* for a more extended critique of this idea.

4   These take many different forms, but in England and Wales they are either part of the Dual System set up in 1944 or are free schools or academies.

5   The committees are called *Agreed Syllabus Conferences* and every local authority is required to have one.

6   Matthew Clayton , Andrew Mason, Adam Swift, & Ruth Wareham, *How to regulate faith schools* (London: Philosophy of Education Society of Great Britain, 2018).

7   Matthew Clayton, et al., *How to...* pp 17 and 26.

8   See Trevor Cooling, 'Formation and Christian Education in England' in Ros Stuart-Buttle and John Shortt (Eds.) *Christian Faith, Formation and Education* (London: Palgrave Macmillan, 2017) for further development of this point.

9   For example Trevor Cooling, *A Christian Vision...*; Elmer Thiessen, *Teaching for Commitment: Liberal Education, Indoctrination and Christian Nurture* (Leominster: Gracewing, 1993); Signe Sandsmark, *Is World View Neutral Education Possible and Desirable?* (Carlisle: Paternoster Press, 2000); Brian Hill, *Exploring Religion in School: A National Priority* (Adelaide: Open Book Publishers, 2004); Doug Blomberg, *Wisdom and Curriculum: Christian Schooling after Postmodernity* (Sioux Center, Iowa: DORDT College Press, 2007); Trevor Cooling et al., *Christian Faith in...*; David I Smith, *On Christian Teaching: Practicing Faith in the Classroom* (Grand Rapids, MI: Eerdmans, 2018).

10 Lynn Revell & Rosemary Walters, *Christian Student RE teachers, Objectivity and Professionalism* (Canterbury: Canterbury Christ Church University, 2010); Ruth Flanagan, 'Implementing a Ricoeurian lens to examine the impact of individuals' worldviews on subject content knowledge in RE in England: a theoretical proposition', *British Journal of Religious Education*, published online (9th October 2019);and Trevor Cooling, Doing God....

11 *www.canterbury.ac.uk/education/our-work/research-enterprise/national-institute-christian-education-research/national-institute-for-christian-education-research.aspx*

12 GCSE is the public exam taken by students in their final year of secondary schooling.

13 Trevor Cooling et al., Christian Faith in...pp. 77-80.

14 Ofsted is the inspection agency for schools in England.

15 The school was a joint Church of England and Catholic school.

16 An influential book was Luke Bretherton, *Hospitality as Holiness: Christian Witness Amid Moral Diversity* (London: Ashgate, 2006).

17 Trevor Cooling, 'Formation...'.

18 See Trevor Cooling, *Christian Faith...* pp. 56-59.

19 Robert A. Bowie 'Interpreting Texts More Wisely: A Review of Research and the Case for Change in English Religious Education' in Ros Stuart-Buttle and John Shortt (Eds.), *Christian Faith, Formation and Education* (Chan, Switzerland: Palgrave Macmillan, 2018) pp.211-228.

20 Robert A. Bowie, and Richard Coles, 'We reap what we sew: perpetuating biblical illiteracy in new English Religious Studies exams and the proof text binary question', *British Journal of Religious Education* 40:3, (2018) pp.277-287.

21 Umberto Eco, *The Role of the Reader: Explorations in the Semiotics of Texts.* (Bloomington, Indiana: Midland Book, 1979) pp.7-11.

22 Robert Bowie, Farid Panjwani, and Katie Clemmey, *Texts and Teachers: The Findings Report* (Canterbury: NICER, 2020) and Robert Bowie (ed.), *Texts and Teachers: The Practice Report* (Canterbury: NICER, 2020). Available at *www.canterbury.ac.uk/nicer/hermeneutics*

23 Margaret Carswell interviewed by Robert A. Bowie, *A message wrapped in words: teaching the Bible in schools,* 2020 (available at youtu.be/MOx_Dcnu04o).

24 Trevor Cooling, 'The Challenge of Passionate Religious Commitment for School Education in a World of Religious Diversity', *Journal of Education and Christian Belief 11:1 (2007), pp. 23-34. See also the RE Council code for teachers at www.religiouseducationcouncil.org.uk/resources/documents/a-practice-code-for-teachers-of-re/*

25 Brian Walsh, 'Transformation...'.

26 *www.churchofengland.org/sites/default/files/2017-10/2016%20Church%20of%20 England%20Vision%20for%20Education%20WEB%20FINAL.pdf*

5
Personal Reflections

This chapter is comprised of three autobiographical reflections that illustrate the impact of worldview reflection on academic development. We conclude in this way because a key theme that has emerged in this report is the significance of the interaction between personal and organised worldviews in RE. This relationship is the nub of the hermeneutical process that is at the heart of learning in RE. It is both the basis of an academically rigorous approach to RE, and the potential platform for the transformative nature of the learning experience. To illustrate the transformative, and academically robust, educational power of the worldview concept, we conclude with an autobiographical finale where Farid, Bob and I will each reflect on its influence in our own academic and personal religious lives.[1] We hope they serve as living examples of how a worldview approach might enrich RE.

Farid – In search of the Simurgh

> Farid is Professor and Dean of the Faculty of Education in the Aga Khan University and was, until recently, Associate Professor in Education and Religion at University College, London. He was a commissioner on the Commission for RE between 2016 and 2018.

As a child, I attended non-formal religious education in my community centre in Pakistan. In a year 4 textbook, we were asked to be grateful to God for giving us water, sunlight and air. This obligation did not make sense to me. Without these conditions, there would be no life – and surely not human life as we know it. I could understand being grateful for having my limbs or good eyesight, as I could imagine myself being deprived of them while still being who I was, but I could not understand being thankful for the fundamental necessities of human existence. Fortunately, my teachers (I asked several!) tried to defend the textbook and persuaded me to accept what was written. I say fortunate, because I was not convinced. Rather, that small crack in the social imagination into which I was being raised initiated a lifelong interest in matters of theology, philosophy, and later, also in education.

This interest remained peripheral for years, reflected mainly in occasional social conversations, almost always within the acceptable boundaries of religious discourse – boundaries which were growing narrower and less tolerant as the country passed through a phase of Islamisation, initiated by Bhutto (d.1977) and crystallised by General Zia (d.1988). Growing up in this atmosphere meant conscious and subconscious adoption of a particular understanding of Islam which was political, essentialist, selective in favour of conservative forces, and increasingly militant in the wake of the Afghan War of the 1980s. One saving grace was that I belonged to a minority denomination within Islam which, despite the national mood, struggled to give its children a more pluralistic, modernist, albeit an essentialist, understanding of Islam.

Like most students at that time, my career choices were hierarchical and almost scripted, with medicine and engineering at the apex and business studies a close second. With those limited choices, I ended up with a degree in business administration. But that small voice inside me calling for theological discussions remained alive, and when, in 1994, an opportunity came to study Islamic Studies in London, I decided to switch career and follow the call of my heart.

In London, I encountered an academic approach to the study of Islam. The next few years were a mixture of cognitive excitement and phases of emotional distress, as so many of my long cherished theological and historical assumptions about Islam and religion needed to be rethought during the course of the journey – a situation reminiscent of Attar's famous poem *Mantiq-ut-Tayr* (the Conference of the Birds).[2] This poem is often interpreted as a quest narrative for self-actualisation in which hundreds of birds search for a king, Simurgh. In Iranian mythology and literature, Simurgh is associated with several ideals including those of healing, saviour, and perfection.

During my studies, my received ideas about Islam, its beliefs and its history were never made the object of direct study in the classroom, and this helped me not to become overly defensive about them. There was no polemics – simply an exposure to other possibilities, and an expansion of my imagination. I recall the fear and trembling as I read *Muhammad: His Life Based on the Earliest Source* by Martin Ling – a convert to Islam – as part of my course on Sira (life of the Prophet).[3] It forced recognition that the religious narratives I cherished had other versions. What I had been taught was a particular selection from the tradition. This helped make sense of the differing claims of various Muslim denominations – but it caused existential angst as the comfort of certainty began to disperse, like sand through a closed fist. Retrospectively, I think, the experience may not be too dissimilar to that of al-Ghazali (d.1111) who in his book *al-Munqidh min al-Dalal* (deliverance from error) gives an account, though contested by modern scholarship, of his spiritual journey, the struggles of his inner life and his crisis of faith.[4] We were exposed to both social scientific as well as theological ways of studying Islam, resulting in an ongoing creative tension between these two modes.

Taking religious plurality seriously is no easy matter. Reading Tabari, a ninth century scholar, helped me understand that religious history is contested with different accounts of events competing for entry into official narrative. Reading EH Carr's *What is History*? began to provide a theoretical framing to the process I was observing in primary texts from Muslim history.[5]

The question of diversity, both inter and intra-religious, remains a central concern in my scholarly work. It poses many questions: philosophical, about the nature of truth; sociological, about social and political impact of deeply entrenched diversity in a society; moral, about the ontological status of ethics; and, historical, about the nature of change and tradition. Islamic studies became the springboard for wider readings around these questions, a case study in the humanities, filling my life with breathtaking moments struggling with Kant, Ibn al-Arabi, Wittgenstein, Ibn Khaldun, Attar, Kierkegaard, and many others.

One of the most important underlying assumptions I imbibed growing up was the belief that religious solutions or responses to any problem can be found by following methodological steps of Muslim jurisprudence. The conventional belief is that sacred texts have meanings in themselves which can be found by the application of the right interpretive method. This right interpretive method can involve linguistic skills, understanding of context and, in some cases, need for a piety and for proper character traits. The human person reading the text is seen as the instrument which needs to be in a perfect shape to arrive at the correct meaning.

Engagement with the theories of hermeneutics has gradually led me to recognise that the notion of "meaning in itself" of religious texts (indeed, of any text) awaiting discovery is hard to sustain. In particular, philosophical hermeneutics associated with Heidegger and Gadamer showed that the historically situated human consciousness of the reader is a necessary element, and not a distraction to be overcome, in the meaning making process. Between Heidegger and Gadamer, we see a key turning point in the hermeneutical tradition. One that recognised that hermeneutics was as much as about the readers as it was about the text. But, if there was no 'meaning in itself' there was no religion in itself too. Rather, various potentials of religious texts, including religiously inspired social critique, were realised through people's interpretation which themselves were hugely shaped by their historically situated consciousness.

The critique of essentialist conceptions of religion opened another realm of investigation as well. Writings of WC Smith, Talal Asad and others showed that the very category of religion needs to be problematised for it emerged "in large measure in the context of Christian attempts to achieve a coherence in doctrines and practices, rules and regulation".[6] More recently, Brent Nongbri (2013) and others have critiqued the 'naturalness' of the term religion which led to the assumption that it is the same across cultures.[7] As the colonial origins of an essentialist image of Islam became clear, I became interested in postcolonial studies. So many of the tropes about religion and Islam that emerged in the nineteenth century have stayed with us, and the work to critically engage with them - a process often called decolonisation – is now gaining momentum. Aspects of this intellectual movement are now increasingly informing my work and outlook.

Every religion is internally diverse. The essentialist academic approaches, which have come under criticism in recent decades, could not negotiate with such diversity, often sliding into the hierarchical mode of orthodoxy and heterodoxy.[8] A hermeneutical approach, which sees meaning making as an ongoing process, helps us make sense of religious diversity without falling into the trap of privileging one theological position over others. This makes it suitable for teaching about religions in non-confessional contexts.[9]

Looking back, it seems that unfulfilled childhood curiosity, non-polemical acquaintance with religious diversity, and engagement with the humanities have been the key variables shaping my unfinished search for the *Simurgh.*

Bob – the humanity-aniac

> Bob is Professor in Religion and Worldviews Education at Canterbury Christ Church University and Director of the National Institute for Christian Education Research.

I grew up in a North London multiethnic Catholic community (Church and schools), but my parents were British converts to Catholicism. At school, I was one of only a couple of students in my class with parents born in Britain. The family household had none of the ethnic, cultural trappings commonly associated with migrant Catholic communities, but it did have fruitful theological conversation – my mother was a Lay Catechist (working with both children and adults), deeply theologically educated in the recent Church developments of Vatican II. The message of lay-led Catholic leadership was strong, and discussion about the nature of the incarnation was a teatime topic. I vividly remember one conversation between my mother and the Parish priest on the steps the Church after Mass. Mum was correcting the priest on where he had gone wrong. It was a lesson in voice and agency.

My *imaginal* landscape was shaped by the science fiction of Isaac Asimov, Robert A. Heinlein, Arthur C. Clarke, the fantasy of Tolkien as well as the wider literature I read and studied, especially as part of my English lessons at school. My Jesuit north London comprehensive school education also introduced me to Ignatian Spiritual Exercises outside of class. I encountered texts in an entirely different way from the practices used in classrooms or pews.[10] It was much more like a meditative encounter – dialogue rather than debate. Once that door opened, a different world opened up. I was to go on to develop these practices, experimenting with silence in formal religious retreats and long-distance walking, and later faltering attempts at Zazen, having read about Zen Buddhist Catholics. I think the mind stretching that these practices and narratives required meant that I later was able to conceive of realities in different ways and it also influenced my understanding of spirituality and sacramentality.

I fell in love with humanities at school, especially Classics, History and English and, in 1990, Classical Civilisation with Philosophy at the University of Warwick allowed me to pursue them all. It was a conscious decision to remain broad, but perhaps also reflected indecision about focus. On top of day classes, I discovered an evening certificate course on the Westwood Campus in Religious Studies. Warwick did not have a Religious Studies department, but Westwood meant I read Ninian Smart, learnt about other religions, and did some textual studies. One session I remember from that time introduced me to the power of metaphor. It was a class discussion of Atman and whether, at the end of this life, it was a case of a single droplet entering into the shimmering sea or the shimmering sea entering into the single droplet. I learnt later on that I had drifted into the range of the Warwick Religions Unit.

My night classes impacted on day class subject choices. I took Julian the Apostate, the story of the Pagan Emperor who ruled after Rome had Christianised, and focused my dissertation on Pre-Christian, Romano-British, Iron Age Religion. I also petitioned Professor Roger Trigg to run a dormant Philosophy of Religion option course.

There was a religious and political life to university study. The ecumenical chaplaincy and student Christian societies brought me into contact with other Christians: Anglicans, Methodists, (Open) Plymouth Brethren and Evangelicals. I became chair of the Student Christian Movement (SCM) with a committee with members of each of these groups. SCM had a political side as well as the prayerful one, with invited speakers debating topics like Third World Debt, oppression in Latin America, the ecological movement and sexual ethics. I remember renowned psychologist Dr Jack Dominion challenging his own Catholic tradition's approach to sexuality on the grounds of psychology and theology in front of a packed university chaplaincy audience at one SCM event. His professional experience of relationship counselling reframed his theological understanding of marriage. There was in this a sense of boundaries shifting and re-clarifying.

The ecumenical project was central to chaplaincy life, marked by visits to the Taizé Ecumenical International Community in France, to which I have continued to return throughout my life. Those opportunities to work, live, study, and pray within a community with young people from all over the world taught me that language was not merely a matter of translation but a dialogue and encounter between different horizons, and that provisionally we could live together producing dynamic possibilities. Roger Schütz, the community's founder, wrote of this dynamic in the provisional nature of the community, confounding ideas that communities must necessarily be dogmatically singular in their own integrity but could instead practice together.[11] I learnt of the coming together of horizons within community before I found Thiselton.[12] I was also being exposed to a community with a pedagogy influenced by the hermeneutics of Paul Ricœur.

Education was a community as well as a personal project. The thousands of young people who gathered to pray together, work together and discuss together, brought tales from many corners of the world, including many former Communist countries. The iron wall across Europe was collapsing. Student groups travelled into former Soviet countries for ecumenical meetings in Prague and Budapest requiring long coach journeys across borders that had very recently been guarded by tanks and machine-gun posts. It was a moment of hope.

Back at the university, the Catholic chaplain of the time had run into difficulties with the local Bishop who thought he was overly ecumenical, which led to a change in personnel. I had a full-blown falling out with the new chaplain on a matter of conscience. I had been deeply influenced by Jesuits and my mother on the primacy of conscience, and this moment of crisis marked the beginning of an adjustment to my religious self-understanding.

The more non-formal educational strand then flipped into the formal study of Religious Studies at Lancaster, which let me add political, feminist and contemporary theologies, sociology (especially Zygmunt Bauman), and some New Testament Studies. In the postgraduate common room, lively debates would break out between Deborah Sawyer, Patrick Sherry, Paul Heelas, Paul Morris, Geoff Clayton, Andrew Shanks and Linda Woodhead at the 10:40am coffee break. The ensuing unofficial seminars would go on for hours.

Education slips from formal to non-formal again, as I left Lancaster to work in Istanbul and then Japan, which I saw as my fifth and sixth years of higher education. I learnt of forms of Islam and Buddhism unlike those I had read about in books. Through intercultural encounters, I leant a lot about the power of language to shape what, much later, I came to realise was something like a worldview. When we encounter the strange, we look to find commonalities, equivalents for the things that we do, and sometimes these are distorting misidentifications, driven by a desire for a shared sense of humanity rather than an appreciation of the different.

Looking back on these influences, I now think that we learn to read reality in a way that shapes how we think – not just how we communicate – at an early age. It matters to learn about both your own *language* (lest you think your perception was the only account of reality) and *languages* of others, so you acquire good habits to speak with them. It is an exercise in dethroning yourself, and I find it very difficult to do.

Through 'non-formal' curricula activities that punctuated my academic life, a symbolic and metaphorical landscape was being built, in which the contours and forms of meaning and significance were shaped into an interpreting prism of the sum of experience so far. The brushes with politics, run-ins with authority, connections with people, especially fondly remembered teachers, and the emotional landscape that matched these remain with me. These contextual factors in how I read reality were clarified through an encounter with hermeneutics. In 1997 as part of the Catholic Certificate in Religious Studies, which I followed at St Mary's, Twickenham, I was given *How to Read the New Testament* by Etienne Charpentier with its diagram of the process of the development of the New Testament.[13] That picture made visible and concrete the layers of meaning captured in words for the first time.

This is a partial reading of my intellectual and spiritual formation, the components selected as an explanation of how I came to end up as a Professor in Religion and Worldviews Education. It is, of course, an attempt to provide an integrated account that makes sense to me and is no doubt in part a projection and reconstruction to create a narrative that is satisfying (at least to me).

Trevor – the unsettled scientist

Trevor is Emeritus Professor of Christian Education at Canterbury Christ Church University and Chair of the Religious Education Council of England and Wales.

My first degree was in the natural sciences during which I accumulated vast amounts of knowledge, but thought little about the nature of that knowledge. In retrospect I realised that the view that I unconsciously absorbed through my experience of science was what can be called positivist realism, whereby I simply assumed that the world was exactly as I saw and experienced it. And that was how I held my Christian faith as well. Truth was what I read in the pages of Scripture (or at least what I was told that I read there by my Christian gurus), and what I learnt in the science laboratory and lecture theatre. And it was all universal, true for everyone. The notion of personal interpretation in either science or Christian faith never crossed my mind.

It was therefore my good fortune to have the opportunity to study a course on the philosophy of science as part of my science degree. That was where I came across Thomas Kuhn's notion of scientific paradigms.[14] It then dawned on me that human understanding of truth could be debatable – and, indeed, could change. My assumed, common-sense realism might actually be naïve. I was introduced to Imre Lakatos' notion of a scientific research programme, which was his attempt to square the circle between Kuhn's seemingly subjective paradigm notion and Karl Popper's more objective idea of falsification being the key way that theories are tested in science.[15] I even found out that there are anarchic philosophers who thought that science was an entirely human construction.[16] Maybe what I thought were literal, objective descriptions of reality might be fictions of the human mind? I had never before realized there was so much discussion around what constituted knowledge in science.

One of the most formative encounters for both my intellectual and my Christian development was with Lesslie Newbigin's work, the missionary bishop of South India, who alerted me to Michael Polanyi's ideas about personal and tacit knowledge.[17] Polanyi was a Hungarian born polymath who gave up a promising career in physical chemistry to take a chair in social sciences at the University of Manchester in order to explore the nature of scientific knowledge. His motivation was to challenge the prevailing positivist view of science, which, given his experience of living under both the Communists and the Nazis, he saw as dangerous in its tendency to totalitarian attitudes supported by over-confidence in one's own knowledge. One of his core arguments was that as humans, scientists approach the task of knowing as inhabitants of what he called a "fiduciary framework", by which he meant a framework of beliefs and attitudes drawn from their learning, background and experience – many of which may be subconscious or, to use his term, tacit. That means that humans often "know more than we can tell". Polanyi was the final nail in the coffin of my naïve scientific realism. I was persuaded that knowledge is personal, framed by a person's fiduciary framework.[18] The totalitarian threat that worried Polanyi comes from a universalising approach to rationality that fails to recognise the personal dimension in knowledge and the resulting imposition of particular fiduciary frameworks in the name of a believed neutral, scientific rationality.

None of these authors used the word *worldview*. Instead they wrote of scientific research programmes, paradigms, fiduciary frameworks, personal and tacit knowledge. Their ideas profoundly influenced my early development as an academic scientist. Essentially they were all advancing the worldview idea even though that language had not become widespread when I first encountered them.

However, my life in academic science was not sealed off from my life as a young Christian. I grew up immersed in the evangelical tradition of the Christian faith. The 1966 Billy Graham evangelistic campaign was a highlight of my teenage years; singing rousing choruses with 90,000 people in Wembley stadium is not something one forgets. In 1974, I ran the university-wide mission for the Christian Union at Cambridge, an initiative that incidentally led to the conversion of Justin Welby, now Archbishop of Canterbury. In my first post as a biology teacher I found myself timetabled to teach RE as I was known to be a church-goer. (I was also timetabled to teach netball, but I have no idea why that happened!) My challenge was to reconcile this evangelical Christian commitment, with my role as a secondary school teacher of both RE and science.

It was during my masters and doctoral studies that the notion of Christian worldview as developed in the Christian Reformed tradition came to my attention.[19] There were many influential authors, but names like Abraham Kuyper, Arthur Holmes, Nicholas Wolterstorff, Brian Walsh, Richard Middleton, Al Wolters, David Naugle, James Sire, Elmer Thiessen, Ruth Deakin, Craig Bartholomew and Michael Goheen regularly figured in the bibliographies of my writing. What these authors convinced me of was that the diversity of belief in the world was not just down to truth and error, but to the fact that human beings interpret their experience of the world differently.

On its own however, this notion of worldview left me with a problem as a teacher. What should be my response be, as a Christian RE teacher, to the diversity of worldviews that I now realized were part of human life? Should I embrace a pillarised approach, and teach RE in a Christian school leaving others to get on with "their worldview thing" while I did my "Christian worldview thing" in my Christian school? But, what then of the idea that the Gospel message is for all people, not just the Christian gated community? Is there not a Christian calling to spread the good news of Jesus Christ? To see RE as an opportunity for evangelism seemed ethically wrong to me – but was I denying my faith by not taking every opportunity to proclaim the Gospel?[20]

The important missing piece in this jigsaw appeared when I encountered the notion of Christian critical realism.[21] This understanding of Christian knowing affirms the notion of a truth out there to which all humans are accountable, accepts that human knowing is inevitably worldview-framed so is always an interpretation of that reality, but, importantly, acknowledges that a process of critical debate and judgment-making is crucial to the human search for truth. It is neither relativist nor absolutist. Critical realism had one particularly important consequence for my understanding of being a Christian religious educator. It highlighted the priority of the virtue of epistemic humility, by which I mean the importance of learning to listen carefully to others and to be reflexive in how one holds one's own commitment if one is to be a good learner in life. This I came to understand as being central to my work as a Christian RE teacher.

The net result of these lifelong deliberations (much simplified here) is that I still identify as an evangelical Christian, but I hold my faith in a very different way from my early evangelical days before my discovery of the notion of worldview. This has enabled me to understand that responsible Christian influence is about helping pupils to understand a diversity of worldviews, about encouraging them to develop epistemic humility in these studies, about supporting them in understanding and taking responsibility for their own personal worldview development whilst being appropriately open about my own Christian worldview in ways that respect the developing autonomy of the pupils.

Conclusion

These three reflective autobiographies have, I hope, illustrated the dynamic interaction between academic study, personal worldview and our development as human beings. They show how we have each experienced the interaction Kueh's three categories of knowledge (substantive content, disciplinary knowledge or ways of knowing and personal knowledge) in different but transformative ways that have shaped each of our personal worldviews. What emerges is the notion that both organised and personal worldviews are a dynamic interplay of fuzzy boundaries and precious, passionately held beliefs. These autobiographies embody the interaction of community influence, upbringing and personal decision-making. They show how immersion in the academic can have a huge impact on one's life. They illustrate the centrality of hermeneutics and of encounters with diversity in the task of learning, both as an academic enterprise and as a personal life project. They capture the notion of bricoleur as we have each described our personal navigation through encounters with diversity. They encapsulate the importance of our responses to critical moments in our lives. Our three journeys tell the story of lifelong interactions with different expressions of organised religion. Our aspiration is that through RE, students, be they religious or not, have the experience of similarly inspiring learning. The fear of some is that to embrace personal development in RE is to damage the academic rigour of the subject. Our testimony is that the opposite is true.

1 Autobiographical reflection is increasingly used in academic writing. See for example Ina ter Avest (ed), *On the Edge: (Auto) biography and Pedagogical Theories on Religious Education* (Rotterdam: Sense Publishers, 2012).

2 Afkham Darbandi and Dick Davis, *The Conference of the Birds* [Original *Mantiq ut-Tayr* by Farid ud-din Attar] (London: Penguin Classics, 1984).

3 Martin Lings, *Muhammad: His Life Based on the Earliest Sources* (London: The Islamic Texts Society, 1983).

4 Montgomery Watt, *The Faith and Practice of Al-Ghazali* (Original Munqidh min al-Dalal by Al-Ghazali) (London: George Allen and Unwin, 1953).

5 E.H. Carr, *What is History?* (London: Penguin, 1964).

6 Talal Asad, *Genealogies of Religion* (Baltimore, USA: Johns Hopkins University Press, 1993), p. 29.

7 Brent Nongbri, *Before Religion: A History of a Modern Concept* (New Haven: Yale University Press, 2013).

8 Shahab Ahmed, *What is Islam?: The Importance of Being Islamic* (Princeton: Princeton University Press, 2016).

9 Farid Panjwani and Lynn Revell, 'Religious education and hermeneutics: the case of teaching about Islam', *British Journal of Religious Education*, 40:3 (2018), pp. 268-276.

10 Robert Bowie, 'Stepping into the text: How the Jesuits taught me to read the bible' in Angela Voss and Simon Wilson (Eds.), *Re-enchanting the Academy* (Waitakere, New Zealand: Rubedo Press, 2017), pp. 139-156.

11 Roger Schütz, *The Dynamic of The Provisional/Dynamique du provisoire*, (Taizé, France: Les Presses de Taizé, 1965).

12 Anthony Thiselton, *New Horizons in Hermeneutics* (Grand Rapids, Michigan: Zondervan, 1992).

13 Etienne Charpentier, *How to Read the New Testament* (London: SCM Press, 1982).

14 See chapter 1.

15 Imre Lakatos, 'Falsification and the methodology of scientific research programmes' in Imre Lakatos and Alan Musgrave, *Criticism and the Growth of Knowledge* (Cambridge: University of Cambridge Press, 1970) and Karl Popper, *The Logic of Scientific Discovery* (London: Routledge, 1992).

16 Paul Feyerabend, *Against Method: Outline of an Anarchistic Theory of Knowledge, 4th Ed* (London: Verso, 2010).

17 Michael Polanyi, *Personal Knowledge: Towards a Post-Critical Philosophy* (Chicago: Chicago University Press, 1958), Michael Polanyi, *The Tacit Dimension* (London:

Routledge and Kegan Paul, 1966) and Lesslie Newbigin, *The Gospel in a Pluralist Society* (London: SPCK Publishing, 2004).

18 This didn't mean that Polanyi was a relativist. He still believed in the pursuit of truth through science and was probably a critical realist.

19 My PhD thesis on this challenge appeared in revised form as Trevor Cooling, *A Christian Vision for State Education* (London: SPCK Publishing, 1994).

20 A career working with Christian teachers convinces me this is a dilemma experienced by many. I have written a lot about this e.g. 'The challenge of passionate religious commitment for school education in a world of religious diversity: reflections on Evangelical Christianity and Humanism', *Journal of Education and Christian Belief*, 11:1 (2007) pp.23-34.

21 See for example, Andrew Wright, *Christianity and Critical Realism: Ambiguity, Truth and Theological Literacy* (London: Routledge, 2013). I discuss this in more detail in Trevor Cooling, *Doing God...*

Conclusion

The world religions paradigm has served well for many years – but it needs retiring. It is no longer fit for purpose in four important respects. First, it focuses too much on a narrow spectrum of institutional religious worldviews rather than developing a broader understanding of the role of both organised and personal worldviews in human life. It therefore finds itself forced into an ever-expanding content base that becomes unmanageable as it seeks to accommodate growing diversity. Second, it perpetuates the struggle between the religious and non-religious communities that jostle to get their version of a worldview onto the curriculum. It does not focus enough on the educational needs of the pupils. Third, it does not engage adequately with the real religion and belief landscape, both in the wider world and amongst the pupils that it should be serving. Fourth, it has never resolved the conundrum as to how to manage the relationship between the knowledge learnt and the pupils' development, despite decades of using the slogan "learning about and learning from religion(s)".

The danger is that many people are interpreting the recommendations of the Commission on Religious Education (CoRE) through the world religions paradigm. Therefore, they see the Commission's Report as just adding more and more content to study, and as adopting a purely sociological frame. We have suggested a very different understanding of that Report. In this, the role of interpretation in knowledge and understanding becomes central. Philosophical hermeneutics is therefore the underpinning academic approach in terms of framing the purpose of the subject. Distinction is made between organised and personal worldviews, but the dialogue between them becomes a central pedagogical focus. Humility as an interpreter, rather than mastery as an expert scholar, is the defining virtue required for academic success. Within this framing, many disciplines are drawn upon in the cause of gaining understanding. Good RE can never just be theology or sociology or philosophy or Religious Studies. All are required if pupils are to learn to be wise interpreters. The RE classroom must be a place where pupils are immersed in a multi-disciplinary experience. Above all, and at its best, RE in the worldview paradigm will be a transformational experience.

My expressed hope was that the CoRE Report would be a "game-changer". I believe it is, as this report explains. But it is only the beginning. There is much to be done in interpreting it properly and applying it in classrooms. There is no one correct way of doing that. I have highlighted some of the early responses. Many more will follow, and I look forward to watching that happen over the next decade.

Theos – enriching conversations

Theos exists to enrich the conversation about the role of faith in society.

Religion and faith have become key public issues in this century, nationally and globally. As our society grows more religiously diverse, we must grapple with religion as a significant force in public life. All too often, though, opinions in this area are reactionary or ill informed.

We exist to change this

We want to help people move beyond common misconceptions about faith and religion, behind the headlines and beneath the surface. Our rigorous approach gives us the ability to express informed views with confidence and clarity.

As the UK's leading religion and society think tank, we reach millions of people with our ideas. Through our reports, events and media commentary, we influence today's influencers and decision makers. According to *The Economist*, we're "an organisation that demands attention". We believe Christianity can contribute to the common good and that faith, given space in the public square, will help the UK to flourish.

Will you partner with us?

Theos receives no government, corporate or denominational funding. We rely on donations from individuals and organisations to continue our vital work. Please consider signing up as a Theos Friend or Associate or making a one off donation today.

Theos Friends and Students

— Stay up to date with our monthly newsletter

— Receive (free) printed copies of our reports

— Get free tickets to all our events

£7/ month
for Friends

£4/ month
for Students

Theos Associates

— Stay up to date with our monthly newsletter

— Receive (free) printed copies of our reports

— Get free tickets to all our events

— Get invites to private events with the Theos team and other Theos Associates

£32/ month

Sign up on our website:
www.theosthinktank.co.uk/about/support-us

Recent Theos publications include:

**Faith and Belief on Campus:
Division and Cohesion
Exploring student faith
and belief societies**

Simon Perfect, Ben Ryan
and Kristin Aune

**After Grenfell: the Faith
Groups' Response**

Amy Plender

**"Science and Religion":
the perils of
misperception**

Nick Spencer

**Religion in Public Life:
Levelling the Ground**

Grace Davie

**Forgive Us Our Debts:
lending and borrowing as
if relationships matter**

Nathan Mladin and
Barbara Ridpath

**Dignity at the End of
Life: What's Beneath the
Assisted Dying Debate?**

Andrew Grey

**People, Place, and
Purpose: Churches and
Neighbourhood Resilience
in the North East**

Paul Bickley

**Doing Good: A Future
for Christianity in
the 21st Century**

Nick Spencer

Religious Education in schools is a vital means of ensuring religious literacy in any society – but in the UK, it is under threat. Recent research suggests the public think RE is an unimportant relic, pupils do not enjoy it as much as most other subjects, and secondary school students are withdrawing from taking exams in it. The stark reality is that some radical rethinking is necessary if the subject is to survive at all. It is with this in mind that the 2018 Commission on RE recommended that the subject should be reframed around the notion of "worldviews". In this report, these recommendations – and particularly the notion of "worldviews" – are defended and elucidated, giving a timely and important reflection on what such an important paradigm shift might mean for the future of Religious Education in the UK.

66

Professor Trevor Cooling is Professor Emeritus of Christian Education at Canterbury Christ Church University UK, and Chair of the Religious Education Council of England and Wales (REC). Previously, Trevor worked as a secondary school teacher in biology and religious education, a university theology lecturer, a diocesan adviser and CEO of a Christian Education charity.

Professor Bob Bowie is Director of the National Institute of Christian Education at Canterbury Christ Church University, Executive Chair of the Association of University Lecturers in Religion and Education, an executive officer of the International Seminar on Religious Education and Values and regional editor for the International Journal of Christianity and Education.

Dr Farid Panjwani is Professor and Dean of the Institute for Educational Development, Aga Khan University, Pakistan.

Cover photograph: Juriah Mosin/shutterstock.com

ISBN: 978-1-9996680-4

'THEOS'

9 781999 668044